Teaching
the
BIBLE
in the
Church

Teaching the BIBLE in the Church

John M. Bracke and Karen B. Tye

CHALICE PRESS

ST. LOUIS, MISSOURI

Biblical quotations, unless otherwise marked, are from the New Revised Standard Version Bible, copyright 1989, Division of Christian Education of the National Council of the Churches of Christ in the United States of America. Used by permission. All rights reserved.

Cover design: Elizabeth Wright
Interior design: Hui-chu Wang
Art direction: Elizabeth Wright

This book is printed on acid-free, recycled paper.

Visit Chalice Press on the World Wide Web at
www.chalicepress.com

10 9 8 7 6 5 4 3 2 1   03 04 05 06 07 08

Library of Congress Cataloging–in–Publication Data

Bracke, John M. (John Martin), 1947-
   Teaching the Bible in the church / John M. Bracke and Karen B. Tye.
      p. cm.
Includes bibliographical references.
   ISBN 0-8272-3643-3 (alk. paper)
   1. Bible—Study and teaching. I. Tye, Karen B. II. Title.
BS600.3.B72 2003
220'.071—dc21

2003009723

Printed in the United States of America

*To our students at Eden Seminary
and in the churches,
our partners in learning to teach the Bible.*

Contents

Acknowledgments

It has been said that one's own biography is often an influence in defining the focus of her or his work. Such is certainly the case regarding our work in this book. We are both children of the church and have been taught a deep love of scripture. We are grateful to all of those throughout our journey who have played a part in our continuing love of and commitment to the Bible and its study in the community of faith.

We give special thanks to our students at Eden, who engaged the ideas in this book with thoughtfulness and care and who provided helpful and encouraging reflections as the work evolved. We are especially grateful to Debbie Irving, who read the manuscript in its entirety and offered constructive and useful feedback that served to strengthen the work. We also offer a word of gratitude to the congregations of First Baptist Church, Greenville, South Carolina, and Kirkwood Baptist Church, St. Louis, Missouri, who invited us into their midst to share our ideas and responded with enthusiasm and support. An additional word of thanks goes to the Christian Educators Network, who invited us to present our work at their annual conference and offered opportunity to refine our ideas in dialogue with those who have primary teaching responsibilities in the local church. We also are deeply grateful to our faculty colleagues, the administration, and the Board of Directors of Eden Theological Seminary for their willingness to grant the time and resources that facilitated our writing efforts.

We would be remiss without a word of deep thanks to our spouses, Mary Bracke and Brenton Dodge, whose unflagging support undergirded us throughout the process of writing and the push to meet deadlines. And finally, our deepest and heartfelt thanks to each other and to the gift we received in being able to partner with a colleague in the work of teaching the Bible and helping our students develop a passion for the task. Our own ministries of teaching are ever blessed by this experience.

Introduction

*Bible study is not just an emphasis to be recovered; it is a
revolutionary possibility…Bible study is every bit as important as
preaching; without it, preaching's centrality becomes a positive
hazard.*[1]

The students quickly join us as we begin singing the familiar
song many of us learned in vacation Bible school: "The B-I-B-L-E.
That's the book for me. I stand alone on the Word of God. The
B-I-B-L-E." Their faces reflect their curiosity as to why their
professors begin a class on teaching the Bible in the church with this
childhood memory. They discover the "method in our madness" as
we talk about the many ways the church reflects its deeply held
conviction that its foundational source of authority is this book it
claims as holy text. Even children learn this early through the words
of a simple song.

As Christians we are called "the people of the Book."
Throughout the centuries we have claimed the Bible as central and
authoritative to our life and mission. To know its stories, to hear its
words of wisdom, to wrestle with the truths it offers, and to draw our
identity from its pages have always been at the heart of the Christian
community's journey in faith.

Even with this claim of authority, however, there seems to be
ample evidence in today's church that many persons hardly know or
study the Bible at all. Several years ago a friend of Karen's shared with
her the results of an informal survey he had done in his
congregation. He asked several people to identify the source of some
wisdom sayings he often heard voiced in our culture. To his great
concern, he discovered that the people were unable to distinguish
between a common folk wisdom such as Benjamin Franklin's "God
helps those who help themselves" (which the people he surveyed
thought came from Jesus) and the actual teachings of Jesus, which

clearly point to a God who helps those who are least able to help themselves.

During a faculty trip to Europe, we found ourselves in a church in Geneva, Switzerland, on the Monday after Pentecost. Pentecost is a national holiday in that country, and there were groups of tourists enjoying some sightseeing on their day off. We overheard a young woman who was touring this church with some friends ask the guide at the desk what this Pentecost was. She had never heard of the story in Acts.

We even see this growing biblical illiteracy in seminary students. We teach in a theological school whose students come from local churches all around the country. We have noted that increasingly students come to seminary to prepare for positions of church leadership with little knowledge of scripture, unfamiliar with even the most basic biblical stories. We have heard this same observation voiced by our colleagues in other seminaries. The evidence seems clear to us—biblical illiteracy pervades our churches.

We believe that offering persons opportunities to study the Bible is among the most important activities that needs to take place in any congregation. The life and mission of churches and the meaning of Christian discipleship are grounded in scripture. The Bible is widely held to be the church's primary witness to the God of Israel whom we have come to know decisively in Jesus Christ. In the United Church of Christ, for instance, the scriptures of the Old and New Testaments are understood as "the word of God" and "the rule of Christian faith and practice."[2] The church has long held that engaging the Bible invites an encounter with God, an encounter through which people may discover the gracious love of God, find their lives transformed, and discern ways to participate in God's mission in a broken world.

The book you are about to read grows out of our claim that there is no more important task for church leaders than to offer persons opportunities to encounter the Bible in deep and meaningful ways. It is vital that the Christian community know, tell, and live the narratives that form our identity. We must be preaching and teaching the Bible in the church.

Claiming the central importance of helping persons in the church engage scripture is not enough, however. We need to address the question of *how* this is done. How do we teach the Bible in ways that form and transform persons and the church? The purpose of this book is to address this question and explore some of the answers that have emerged out of our work in both the seminary and the church.

The work that we have done *together* is vital to the insights we share in this book. We believe this cooperative endeavor between a religious educator and a biblical scholar was and continues to be critical, and we offer it as a model to others concerned about vital issues in the life of the church today. Our effort here is more than the sum of our individual contributions, and we trust that it enables us to offer important insights into this central task of the church—teaching the Bible.

Assumptions

Our approach to teaching the Bible is grounded in several beliefs and assumptions that influence the way we engage the question "How do we teach the Bible?" and answer it. First, we believe that the goal of teaching the Bible is transformation, not just information. We live in an "information" culture. One of the growing fields of employment is information systems management. We are hungry for data, for facts, for more and more information. Often we approach Bible study from this perspective, in which the goal is the learning of "facts" about the scriptures. We focus on "who, what, when, where, why, and how." Who was Moses, and when did he live? Did he actually write the first five books of the Old Testament? What was it like to live in Palestine during the time of Jesus? Why did Paul persecute Christians? Where did his missionary journeys actually take him and when? We want the "facts" and think that when we have acquired the information we have engaged the Bible.

Of course, we don't deny that knowing "facts" about the Bible is important. In fact, such information is a critical starting point. It is much easier to study scripture when we know the books of the Bible and their sequence. We believe that it is worthwhile, at an appropriate age, for children to learn the books of the Bible and to memorize some texts. Information about the social, cultural, political, and economic circumstances of peoples in the Bible is also important. Yet we do not believe that churches have really "taught" the Bible by simply conveying information about texts.

Given this key assumption—that the purpose of teaching the Bible is to invite transformation—we submit that studying the Bible involves more than knowing when Moses lived or where Paul may have traveled. Truly encountering scripture is to stand before the God whom Moses served when he dared to say to Pharaoh, "Let my people go!" and having stood before this God, to ask how the God of oppressed slaves may be calling us to serve today. Studying the Bible is more than asking about where Paul traveled and when. Studying the Bible is to hear Paul proclaim that the gospel of Jesus Christ means "there is no longer Jew or Greek...slave or free...male and female" (Gal. 3:28), and then struggle with the meaning of this radical gospel for our time and place. To teach the Bible faithfully is to have transformation as our goal. It is not that we as teachers effect the transformation, but that we invite through the study of scriptures an encounter with God, who empowers transformation—of both teacher and student. One author has captured this transformative character of Bible study like this:

> A characteristic of formational reading is openness to mystery. Instead of the problem solving mentality, instead of coming to what we are reading to find a solution for something else in our life, we come to be open to that Mystery we call God. We come to stand before that Mystery and allow that Mystery to address us.[3]

We assume that teaching the Bible has as its goal not just the conveying of information, but an invitation to transformation, an encounter with "that Mystery we call God."

A second assumption is related to one of our primary concerns in this book, an educational concern involving the process of learning and teaching. We assume that there is a need to teach the Bible in ways that all involved are invited to journey to a new place—a new place of knowing and understanding the Bible, a new place of living before God, a new place in becoming Jesus' disciple, a new place for the church to be part of God's mission.

In order to engage the Bible in these ways, we need to be attentive to the dynamics of learning and teaching. We need to pay attention to the ways in which people learn. We need to explore the brain, our primary organ of learning. Every day researchers are making new discoveries about how the brain learns. We need to be familiar with these discoveries. We need to recognize that persons are different and do not all learn the same way. Thus, an understanding of learning styles is important to the work of teaching.

The dynamics of how the brain learns and an understanding of the different ways in which people learn are factors that skilled teachers always consider in planning their teaching. Too often in our churches, however, we ask people with wonderful commitment but little background or experience to teach. Good intentions help but cannot be a substitute for awareness of and knowledge about how learning and teaching best occur. As we think about teaching the Bible in churches, we believe that attention to the dynamics of learning and the skills of teaching is essential.

A third assumption that informs our approach to teaching the Bible concerns culture. We believe that teaching the Bible in the church is an intercultural educational experience. In order to teach, therefore, we need some understanding of intercultural education and how one teaches and learns across cultures.

Put simply, culture refers to the way of life of a given community or people. Culture includes behavior, speech, traditions, beliefs and values, institutions and their structures, relationships and how they are organized, and ways of thinking and doing things. We believe that the cultures of our modern world and the cultures of biblical times are different. People in each of these contexts speak, behave, believe, relate, and organize their lives in very different ways. In order to engage scripture in meaningful ways, we have to be able to move into another culture, engage it, and learn from it.

This begins with understanding our own culture. Sometimes we make the mistake of thinking that "culture" is what those different from us have. However, we *all* live in a culture but are often unaware of it and the way it shapes us. It has been said that culture is like water to fish. Ask a fish about the water, and it may well respond, "What water?" Like fish so immersed in water they are likely not to see it, so we are immersed in our culture and hardly notice it. Unless we are aware of the cultural lens that we bring to the biblical text, we risk imposing our own cultural viewpoints on the Bible and thereby misunderstanding the text. Such misunderstandings can lead us to distort the meaning of biblical texts.

Not only are we challenged by our own cultural lens, we need to be aware of the layers of cultural perspectives present in any given teaching situation. People who gather to study the Bible in the church are likely to bring different cultural experiences to the task. Although all may belong to the same church, they may have been brought up in a different church tradition and bring that cultural perspective to the conversation. Persons also come from different social positions in the community that carry cultural perspectives— about how wealth or poverty are viewed, for instance. An awareness of these cultural lenses is important, too.

Finally, the Bible itself is the product of cultures that are historically and geographically far removed from us. Notice that we said *cultures* in the plural. The Bible took shape over many hundreds of years, during which time culture changed. When reading the Bible, one encounters many cultures and also different cultures encountering one another. For instance, in the Old Testament, we encounter the late Bronze and early Iron Age Palestinian culture of indigenous Palestinian peoples that soon is in tension with an emerging Israelite culture. In the New Testament, we encounter Roman and Jewish cultures existing in tension. All these cultures have a shaping influence on the texts we read.

In several ways, then, we assume that teaching the Bible is an intercultural experience. As we work at the teaching task in our churches, we need to be attentive to the intercultural dynamics of our work and develop those understandings and skills that enable us to engage in this multilayered task.

A fourth assumption informing our work is the importance of the insights of critical biblical scholarship for teaching the Bible in the church. Over the last two hundred years, scholars have studied the Bible from a variety of perspectives. Some have attempted to understand who wrote biblical texts and the historical and cultural context in which this writing was undertaken. Other scholars have attempted to understand the processes by which the Old and New Testaments as we have them took shape. Others have focused on the biblical text itself and have observed how literary features of a text— for instance, the way a story is told or the way a poem is developed— can contribute to our understanding of a biblical text. Some have observed that often the way we make sense out of a biblical text has to do with who we, as readers of the text, are and what we bring to the text (e.g., our church background, our life experience as men or women or as members of a dominant or minority ethnic group).

The insights of biblical scholarship have much to offer those of us concerned with teaching the Bible in churches. Of course, there is a danger here. We can draw on the resources of biblical scholarship in such a way that we are primarily sharing information about the text rather than engaging the text in a way that might be transformational. We focus on information about the author of a text, the situation in which a text was written, or the larger historical context of that time and never ask how the text witnesses to God or how God encounters us through the text. We know about the way a biblical story uses plot or how a psalm uses the imagery of a thunderstorm but miss the way the text invites us to encounter God.

Although there are certainly pitfalls in using the approaches of scriptural scholars, there is also much to be gained. We need to engage in thoughtful, careful, and informed ways of reading and interpreting texts. Biblical scholarship helps us to do that. Not every meaning we seek to make of a given text is appropriate to that text. Teaching the Bible in the church is an important responsibility, and part of that responsibility is to be intentional about how one makes sense of biblical texts.

These, then, are the assumptions that inform our work with regard to teaching the Bible in the church: (1) It is about transformation, not just information; (2) it calls for knowledge about how the brain works, how people learn, and how we teach for learning and transformation; (3) it is an intercultural experience and calls for an understanding of intercultural education; and (4) it requires an appropriate engagement with and use of critical biblical scholarship. Although we do not claim that these assumptions are exhaustive of the issues we need to address when teaching the Bible, we do believe that these are foundational to such work.

A Road Map to the Book

You can probably anticipate already the topics that we discuss in the chapters that follow. But it is important also to know the way in which we see these topics relate to one another. Figure 1 provides a visual perspective of these relationships. At the heart of the biblical teaching moment are the teacher, student, and text. It is their connecting with one another that offers the moment of possibility for transformational learning to occur. But the teacher, student, and text do not connect in isolation from other factors. Central among these factors and shaping not only the teacher, student, and text but also one another are issues related to (1) learning, (2) teaching, (3) culture, and (4) interpretation.

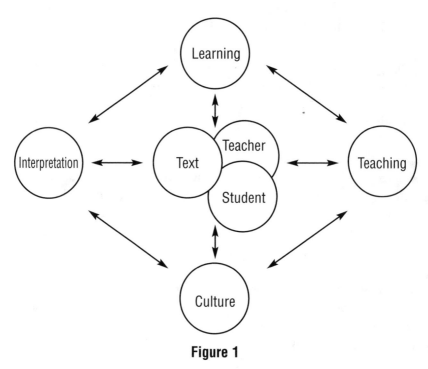

Figure 1

Given this understanding of the teaching moment, we begin in chapter 1 with a discussion of learning and what it is we need to know in order to teach for learning when working with the Bible in the church. Included in this discussion is an introductory exploration of the brain, memory, learning styles, and multiple intelligences. In chapter 2 we move to a discussion of teaching and the kinds of knowledge needed to teach in ways that take seriously our goals of learning and transformation. In chapter 3 we explore the nature of intercultural education and the issues related to culture that play a significant role in how we teach the Bible. In this discussion we look at the impact of our own culture on our engagement with the Bible, the intercultural character of our communities of faith, and the cultural worlds of the Bible. In chapter 4 we consider the role of critical biblical scholarship in teaching the Bible in the church and discuss issues related to biblical interpretation and the choice of intentional reading strategies as they relate to the teaching of scripture. With each of these chapters, we also name important principles for teaching that grow out of the content of the chapter. In the final chapter we invite you to enter a teacher's workshop to see the kinds of decisions teachers need to make when planning to teach the Bible in the church.

Our audience is clearly those who teach in the church. These include pastors, church educators, lay teachers, and those in seminaries preparing for this important work. You are the people on the front lines of teaching the Bible in congregations, people who can make a difference. Our hope is that pastors find this book helpful as they attempt to be faithful to their call to be both pastor and teacher of the congregation. We believe this work is also a resource for educators and lay teachers in the church, those who have accepted the call to the teaching ministry within a congregation. Although published curricula are often used as the primary resource by these teachers, we believe this book will provide background and guidance that allows more effective use of such curricula.

Given the centrality of the Bible in the life of the Christian community and the need to address the growing concern about the biblical illiteracy present in many of our churches, it is important that we give high priority to teaching the Bible in the church. Although this can be a complex and rigorous task, there is none more worthy of our time and energy. May you engage the challenge with hope and faith, trusting that the God we meet in the pages of scripture is the God who guides our efforts.

1

Teaching the Bible: How We Learn

It was the first night of a workshop on teaching the Bible in the church that we were leading for a local congregation. The participants were church school teachers of children and adults and several interested church members. In order to illustrate some of the material we were presenting, we asked the participants to read and think about Psalm 23. After some discussion of early memories regarding this psalm, we invited participants to sit back, close their eyes, and listen to a musical representation of this text. The room became quiet, and slowly the sounds of a beautiful Gregorian-like chant filled the air and the familiar words began: "The Lord is my Shepherd, I have all I need, She makes me lie down in green meadows, Beside the still waters, She will lead."[1] We could feel the mood in the room shift. "She restores my soul, She rights my wrongs, She leads me in a path of good things, And fills my heart with songs." It was almost as though the participants were holding their collective breath. What was this?

Even though I walk, through a dark and dreary land,
There is nothing that can shake me,
She has said she won't forsake me,
I'm in her hand.

She sets a table before me, in the presence of my foes
She anoints my head with oil,
And my cup overflows.

11

Surely, surely goodness and kindness will follow me,
All the days of my life,
And I will live in her house,
Forever, forever and ever.

As the music came to an end, the quiet was absolute. We paused for a moment, then asked for people's responses. Slowly they came. Some were angry—"I don't like that interpretation. The language doesn't speak to me!" "God isn't a She!" "I had a hard time listening." Others were deeply moved, but for different reasons. One person said that the beauty of the music held her attention. Another woman said that it was a deeply emotional experience for her, that she felt a real connection with the psalm because of the feminine language. When we commented that Bobby McFerrin wrote this version of Psalm 23 for his mother and dedicated it to her, we saw faces light up with recognition and understanding. This information seemed to help make a connection with this representation of the text, especially for those who were angry or feeling some discomfort.

In witnessing this encounter, we became aware that we were watching learning take place, watching the process by which people struggle to know, understand, and make meaning of a biblical text, with all its accompanying complexities and ambiguities. Understanding something about this process we call learning is foundational to our work as teachers of the Bible in the church. In this chapter we want to discuss some of the primary factors that we have discovered are key to how people learn. We believe this information is vital if we are to teach the Bible in ways that enable people to learn, make meaning, and hopefully be transformed. Although we cannot engage in an exhaustive look at learning, which would take volumes, we do want to consider some of the basics about learning that have proven helpful to our own work in teaching the Bible. These basics include (1) the brain and how it works, (2) memory and how it is formed, and (3) the role of learning styles and multiple intelligences in the learning process.

The Brain and How It Works

As we observed the participants in our workshop on teaching the Bible that evening, we were observing the human brain at work.

In fact, it is simply impossible to talk about learning without beginning with the brain. However, we need to hear a word of caution. Although neuroscientists are making amazing discoveries regarding how the brain works, there is still so much we do not know. Therefore, we need to approach the following discussion with a certain sense of humility, open to the new discoveries that are yet to come. That does not mean, however, that we don't have several important insights already at hand. As Eric Jensen says, although we do not yet have an "inclusive, coherent model of how the brain works," we do know enough to rethink and reshape how we teach and learn.[2] What are some important "facts" about the brain that we need to know?

First, the human brain is "the best organized, most functional three pounds of matter in the known universe."[3] As human beings, we have more than enough brain matter for the work of learning! Our brains have more than 100 billion neurons, or nerve cells, and these neurons are key to learning. In fact, neuroscientists define learning as "two neurons communicating with each other."[4] Neurons have "learned" when one neuron sends a message and another neuron receives that message. In other words, learning occurs when two neurons communicate. They make a connection. But it is more than just two single neurons. Several neurons become involved in the communication, and what is called a "neural network" is formed. It is the engagement of these neural networks that is central to learning.

The key here is to continually engage these connections. As Marilee Sprenger points out, "The more frequently a neural network is accessed, the stronger it becomes."[5] The more we use the connections that have been made in a neural network, the more firmly set that learning becomes. Let's use an example. A child sees a cat for the first time. Her mother points to the cat and says "cat." The child attempts to repeat the word. At that moment her brain makes a connection. A few neurons are talking about "cats." If the cat meows, the child makes a connection that this object called a cat makes a sound like this. The next time she sees a cat and hears it meow, her brain will make these same connections—cat and meow. Each time the child encounters a cat and hears it meow, the neurons become more efficient at connecting, and the message that this is a cat and it meows travels more swiftly through the neural network. As time goes on, the child will add more connections to the neural network regarding cats; the more this network is used (in other words, the more the child encounters cats), the stronger the connections will be.

Let's return to our participants in the workshop. When we first asked these folks to talk about their early memories and experiences with Psalm 23, we were inviting them to access their neural networks regarding this psalm. Many of them had had several encounters with this very familiar psalm, and therefore some strong connections were already in place. That's how neural networks work. The more we return to a familiar text and read it, hear it in sermons, sing it in songs, encounter it in a variety of settings (funerals are a favorite setting for Psalm 23), the stronger the learning with regard to that text.

Scientists call this strengthening of the neural networks "neural branching." The more we engage an object, experience, or idea, the more connections or "branches" are formed between neurons and the easier it is for that network to be accessed and used. The opposite is also true. When a neural connection is not used, when we no longer have some experiences or encounter certain objects or read about certain subjects or exhibit certain behaviors, the connection is lost. As Sprenger says, "Each day the brain prunes some neuronal connections because of lack of use."[6]

This knowledge that the brain engages in both neural pruning and branching as it makes connections carries an important implication for our work as teachers of the Bible. We can either teach for branching or teach for pruning. We teach for neural branching by helping our students make connections with the material and doing this over and over again. The first time a child hears a Bible story, a connection is formed. A neural network begins to take shape. Whether that network stays in place and the knowledge becomes a part of long-term memory depends a great deal on whether the network is accessed again and again. This is why it is important to focus on a single story and to tell that story over and over again in a variety of ways. Jumping from story to story too quickly, as sometimes happens in some church school curricula, does not aid in the development of neural branching and generally leads to little of that story being retained. By not using the connections again and again, we engage in neural pruning. If our participants in the workshop had only heard Psalm 23 a few times in their lives, their memories of this psalm would be weak. But because of its frequent use in a variety of settings, many of those participants had strong memories, strong neural networks with regard to this particular text.

The knowledge that the brain engages in neural branching and pruning as a part of the learning process leads to another fact we need to know about the brain. Scientists are now talking about the "plasticity" of the brain,[7] referring to the brain's ability to grow and change. We used to think that the brain was pretty well "fixed" by a young age, usually around the age of five, but research is now indicating that this is simply not true. The brain continues to adapt and change throughout our lifetime. We actually change the physical structure of the brain through the experiences we have, meaning that we engage the brain's neural branching and pruning capabilities through our experiences. The old adage "You can't teach an old dog new tricks" is just not true from a brain perspective. We are capable of continuing to learn, of shaping our neural networks, throughout our lives.

We were offering an opportunity for new learning when we played the McFerrin interpretation of Psalm 23 for our workshop participants. Trusting in the brain's plasticity and that new branching could occur, we sought to expand our participants' understandings of Psalm 23 and its meanings for their lives by offering a new experience that held the possibility that a new branch would be formed in their neural network regarding this psalm. We sought to help this connection in a couple of ways. First, by asking participants to share their memories of this psalm, we were activating the networks already in place. Second, in placing this new interpretation in a context by sharing the origins of McFerrin's work as a tribute to his mother, we were providing a way to connect to this different translation with which participants might identify. Our own experiences of mothers as those who shepherd us, love us, and steadfastly stand by us open a neural branching between Psalm 23 and mothers that might deepen our insight regarding the nature of the Lord, or God, and strengthen our neural network for this text.

A third fact about the brain that is important for teachers of the Bible to know is in regard to certain structures of the brain that play a significant role in learning. Our purpose here is not to go into great detail regarding these structures and their specific biology but to help us understand how the brain engages in the work of learning and creating memory. We will say more about memory itself in a later section of this chapter.

Located in a central part of the brain, called by some the limbic brain,[8] are two structures that are crucial to learning and memory. These are the hippocampus and the amygdala (see figure 1). The hippocampus sorts and files the factual information that the brain learns. The amygdala sorts and files emotional information. To understand the importance of these two brain structures, we need to look briefly at how the brain processes information.

Information comes into our brain through our five senses and is first filtered through the brain stem. It is then sent to the thalamus, the brain structure that first sorts information. If the information is visual, the thalamus sends it to the visual part of the cortex, where it is initially processed; if it is auditory, it sends it to the auditory cortex, and so on. The cerebral cortex also sorts through the information, relaying it to the hippocampus for cataloging and filing. The hippocampus does not actually house the information itself. It sends it on for permanent placement in other storage places in the brain and the body.

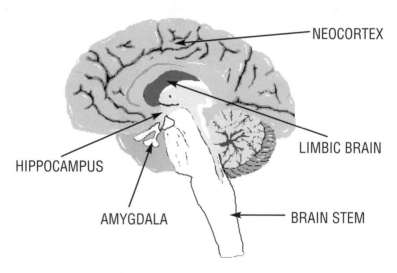

Figure 1

The hippocampus plays an important role in determining what is retained and what is forgotten. The senses continually flood the brain with information, some of it vital but much of it unimportant. You don't need to remember the face of everyone you pass on the street, but you do want to recognize the faces of your spouse and children! To prevent an information overload that would accompany having to remember too much, the hippocampus sifts through the barrage of incoming information from the cortex and picks out what to store and what to discard. In other words, the hippocampus serves as a central clearinghouse, deciding what information will be placed in long-term memory and helping to retrieve it when called upon.

The question that comes to the fore, then, is how the hippocampus decides what is worth storing—in other words, what is worth learning and remembering. There is growing evidence that two primary factors shape the hippocampus's decision to store information for future access. The first is whether the information has emotional significance. The amygdala is the key player in this decision. The second factor is whether the new information relates to something we already know. Put another way, "If information is not meaningful or allowed to form patterns in the brain, it will be lost."[9]

Two important implications for teaching the Bible emerge from this information about how the brain works. The first of these is that emotion plays a significant role in learning. We ignore it at our peril! As Robert Sylwester says, "The best teachers know that kids learn more readily when they are emotionally involved in the lesson because emotion drives attention, which drives learning and memory. It's biologically impossible to learn anything that you're not paying attention to."[10] The relationship between attention and emotion is critical. Our choice to play McFerrin's interpretation of Psalm 23 for our workshop participants was a deliberate one because we knew it would evoke an emotional response from listeners. Not everyone felt the same emotion, but they all had a felt response and were attentive to what was going on. But it wasn't enough just to evoke an emotional connection and have their attention. We also needed to do something with that attention, to engage that emotional response in a positive and helpful way. This leads to the second implication for teaching the Bible that emerges from our understanding of the work of the hippocampus. This is the importance of teaching for connections. As mentioned earlier, the brain is naturally a connecting organism. It engages in neural branching as it processes information. We can help it in this process, and help the hippocampus do its work of sorting information, if we provide some connections between new information and that which is already in place. It is like knowing what file folders are already in the files before we start to put new material in them. We sought to get a feel for the connections that were already in place for our participants by asking them to reflect on early memories they had of Psalm 23: where they had first heard it, some of the important images it evoked for them, and what associations they had with it. In addition, this helped the participants bring these connections into conscious memory.

But we also wanted to help make connections with this new expression of the psalm. To do so, we drew on the context out of which McFerrin's interpretation came—a tribute to his mother. Participants were invited to think about why McFerrin would identify this psalm with his mother, and we found ourselves in the midst of a rich discussion about the similarities between the qualities of a good mother and the qualities of the shepherd in the psalm. It was a short step to begin to think of our images of God and how God might be like a mother. To our mostly city-dwelling participants, who had never seen a sheep or shepherd in their lives except in the movies and therefore had few brain connections in place regarding shepherds, a connection between God and mother held as much promise, if not more, for neural branching as did a connection between God and shepherd. Such connections opened up the possibility for new and richer meaning with regard to this familiar text.

Of course, connections cannot be made at all if we do not have the brain's attention, so we would be remiss in this discussion about how the brain learns if we did not talk briefly about the role that attention plays in all this. One of the important tasks in teaching for learning is getting the brain's attention. It is said that a normal person makes the decision of where to turn his or her attention about 100,000 times a day.[11] So what influences the brain's attention?

We've already talked about the role that emotions play in learning and how emotions drive attention. Making decisions based on emotions is not the exception with the brain, it is the rule. Good teaching does not avoid emotions, but instead embraces them. But there are other influences on attention in learning. The brain is attentive to relevancy, so we need to engage information and present it in ways that are relevant for people. As Renate Caine says, "The best learning happens when necessary facts and skills are embedded in experiences that relate to real life, when there's a big picture somehow."[12] An important question a teacher needs to ask regularly is, How is this pertinent to my students' personal, everyday lives? In asking it we need to be aware that what is relevant to us as teachers may not be relevant to our students, especially if we come from different generations. It is vital that the question is asked from the perspective of the students and what is relevant to their lives.

The brain also becomes attentive when faced with contrast. "If you want attention, provide a strong contrast from what you were just doing."[13] The brain is stimulated by novelty and change. The presentation of material also needs to be engaging rather than passive. Getting people physically involved in the learning process, through conversation, movement, and engagement of various kinds, is key to holding the brain's attention.

A word of caution, however, is needed here. Calling for the brain's constant attention is counterproductive. Research shows that the brain does poorly at continuous, high-level attention. In fact, such attention can be sustained for only a short period, generally ten minutes or less. Information taken in has to be processed, and this requires reflective time on the part of the brain, when the brain's attention is internal and is not focused on acquiring new information. As Eric Jensen says, "You can either have your learners' attention or they can be making meaning, but never both at the same time."[14] Along with stimulating the brain's attention, we also need to provide regular time within our teaching sessions for the brain to reflect, for the learning to "imprint." In a typical teaching setting, this means alternating among input of information, group work, personal reflection time, and individual work. Time for reflection and processing can occur in a variety of ways, including having learners talk for a few minutes in small groups about what they have just heard or read, inviting them to write for a few minutes in a journal or log about what they learned, or providing opportunities for learners to respond through music, art, or movement.

The final fact with regard to the brain that we want to address in this section is the relationship of challenge and the brain's learning processes. The brain is attentive to challenge. As Eric Jensen says, "What the human brain does best is learn,"[15] and challenge is a critical ingredient in this learning. Boredom is more than annoying to the brain. It actually can lead to "thinning," or to that neural pruning about which we talked. When bored, the human brain stops attending, and learning is minimal. Challenge and stimulation are important brain "nutrients." As teachers of the Bible, we need to give thought to ways in which we are challenging our students' brains. We challenge by providing a variety of experiences, by introducing novelty and new ways of thinking and doing, by offering a range of sensory stimulation that engages all five of the senses, by offering choices so the brain engages in decision making, and by providing as enriched an environment as possible for learning.

In addition to understanding how important challenge is to the brain's learning processes, we also need to reflect on the relationship between challenge and threat. In reality there is a fine line between the two, and crossing this line can have significant impact on whether learning occurs. If intellectual challenge is experienced as emotional stress, the brain has a problem learning. When we chose to introduce the McFerrin rendition of Psalm 23 to our workshop participants, we knew that we would need to be sensitive to this issue of challenge and threat. Our invitation to hear and experience the psalm in a new way could easily have become threatening to some. If that happened, the ability to learn would be diminished.

When the brain perceives a threat, it has a range of responses available to it. One of these responses is what is called "downshifting,"[16] in which the "reptilian" brain,[17] that part of the brain concerned with survival, takes over in order to ensure the individual's safety. This part of the brain is not a thinking brain, and access to the brain's higher order thinking and critical reflection skills is diminished when it is in charge. We often comment to each other that we can see downshifting taking place in an individual. It's almost as if the lights go out—their eyes glaze over; the expressions on their faces become rigid and fixed—and we know that the child, youth, or adult is simply working to "survive" the threat they feel to their worldview and well-being. Until we can invite them back into the learning process and out of their downshifted state, not much learning will occur.

One of the important factors in avoiding downshifting is to provide a sense of safety for our learners. When it comes to establishing an optimal environment for learning, the place to begin is by removing threats and fear from the learning setting. Seldom does threat take the form of physical violence in the settings where we teach the Bible, but there are other threats that can impact learning. These include a threat to a long-established worldview and the threat of embarrassment, humiliation, sarcasm, unrealistic demands, failure, and so on.

Safe space is critical to helping people feel challenged rather than threatened. We tried to provide safe space for our workshop participants by giving them the freedom to respond to the McFerrin piece in whatever way they chose. We sought to communicate that it was okay not to like it or to find it meaningful. By introducing the context out of which the piece was written, we hoped to offer a "safe" way to hear the psalm and understand why it might have been expressed that way. The language was less threatening when it was seen as a tribute to a mother. Guarding against threat while challenging our students' brains is an important task for those of us who teach the Bible.

To summarize, knowledge about the brain and how it works is vital for teachers of the Bible. Understanding that brains are naturally learning organs designed to make connections provides us with helpful insight as we design our teaching experiences. Knowing that the brain can change, learn new ways and new ideas, offers hope that our teaching efforts are not in vain. Realizing the important role that emotion plays in all of learning and knowing how emotion drives attention gives us vital information for engaging our students' attention and helping the brain make meaning and form lasting memories. Appreciating the relationship of challenge and threat to the brain's processing of information enables us to make decisions about our learning environments that will significantly impact the learning process. From this brief overview of some basic facts about how the brain works, let us turn our attention now to the issue of memory—how it is formed—and its role in learning.

Memory and How It Is Formed

"Learning and memory are two sides of a coin to neuroscientists. You can't talk about one without the other. After all, if you have learned something, the only evidence of the learning is memory."[18] We believe that it goes without saying that those of us who teach the Bible want our students to remember what they have been taught! So what do we know about memory and how it is formed that can be helpful to our work as teachers of the Bible?

First, another word of caution. As with other discoveries regarding the brain and how it works, science has made tremendous strides in recent years in the exploration of memory, what it is, and how it functions. But this is still "frontier" work, and there is much yet to be discovered. That does not mean, however, that there are not important insights from the research on memory that are very useful to those of us called to be teachers in the church.

Let's begin with a definition of what memory is. Jerry Larsen, in his book *Religious Education and the Brain,* defines memory in this way: It is "the totality of experiences, information, skills, meanings, and models we and our culture have designed together and have deposited in the neural pathways of the cortex."[19] The important point Larsen seeks to make is that memory is more than information or a collection of data. It is a complex web of experiences, information, feelings, and behaviors that enables us to connect new data and experience, make choices and decisions, and fashion meaning for our lives.

Biologically, memory is a persistent change in the brain created by a transient stimulus.[20] Basically, memory is a process rather than a fixed thing. It is a process by which persistent connections—those neural networks—are formed. So how does this process work?[21]

As seen in figure 2, the process begins with stimuli being received in the sensory register. These stimuli are both conscious and unconscious, and there are literally millions of them per second. If we were structured to remember them all, we would be so overwhelmed that it would be impossible to function. But only a small portion of these millions of stimuli—mainly those to which we pay some attention—are placed in *short-term memory*, a temporary storage buffer lasting anywhere from five to twenty seconds. If we engage in some form of active processing of the stimuli—such as repeating it, thinking about it, discussing it, and so on—it moves to *working memory*. Working memory is of limited capacity and can last up to several hours. It is possible through repetition and concentration to hold stimuli in working memory long enough to pass a test, which is why cramming for exams does work but leads to only temporary retention of the information. To move the stimuli to *long-term memory* requires active processing that goes beyond just repetition and a few moments of reflection. Continual elaboration, repetition, practice, reflection, and connection are key to creating long-term memory. We will say more about this later in this section.

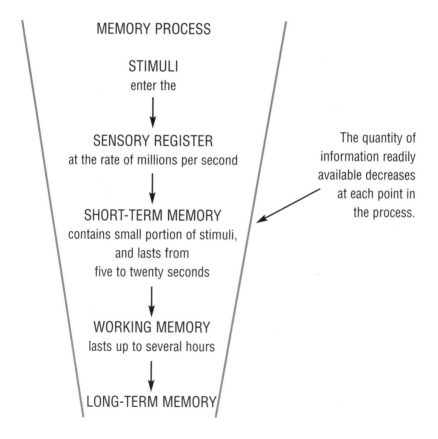

Figure 2

To summarize, the process of creating memory goes something like this: A stimulus is received in the sensory register and moves to short-term memory, from there to working memory, and finally to long-term memory, where information is kept for an indefinite period. It is important to note that the quantity of information available to the learner decreases as it moves through this process. In other words, we receive much more information than we ever keep for long-term access. One of the hopes for teaching is that we can learn to provide information, or stimuli, in ways that will assist in more of it being remembered and accessible throughout our students' lives.

If our goal is to teach for long-term memory, it is helpful to have some understanding of the long-term memory system. This understanding begins with the realization that "long-term memory" does not refer to a collection of data stored in a single location in the brain. Rather, when we talk about long-term memory, we are talking about an interconnected web of neural networks. In fact, memories are not only kept in the brain, they are also kept throughout the body.

The use of the phrase "long-term memory *system*" is helpful here because it reminds us that we are indeed dealing with a *system,* an interconnecting web of neural networks. Within these networks are different types of memory, and, as Jerry Larsen points out, "most things that become lasting memories are a combination of several (sometimes *all*) of these kinds of memory."[22] If we want to teach for long-term memory, then we want to teach in ways that engage these different memory types.

Various authors who write about the brain and memory name these types of memory in slightly different ways. We have found the typology developed by Marilee Sprenger[23] to be particularly helpful in our thinking about memory and the work of teaching the Bible. Sprenger names five memory types: semantic, episodic, procedural, automatic, and emotional.

Semantic memory holds information learned from words. It is sometimes called linguistic memory. This memory type includes names, facts, and information from textbooks and lectures. Although we may not call what we do in church a lecture, we still talk "at" people a lot in sermons and Bible studies. Most church schools rely heavily on semantic memory with the use of printed curriculum resources such as booklets and pamphlets we have our students read. We are often awash in words in our teaching contexts. The problem with semantic memory is that it requires several repetitions of the information in order for it to become established in this memory bank. And even then, this particular memory can fail us unless we are able to draw on connections, associations, contrasts, and what Larsen calls "hooks"[24] into the other memory types available to us.

MEMORY PROCESS

Semantic memory	Also called linguistic memory. Holds information learned from words. Requires several repetitions to be retained.
Episodic memory	Also called contextual or spatial memory. Retains location, context, and circumstance. Requires no practice, forms quickly, seldom fails us.
Procedural memory	Also called muscle memory. Retains actions and behaviors. Easily stored and recalled.
Automatic memory	Also called conditioned response or reflexive memory. Relies on instant associations. Requires constant repetition and memorization.
Emotional memory	The most powerful memory, taking precedence over other memory types. Relies on emotional associations related to information and experience. Providing emotional "hooks" is key.

Figure 3

Episodic memory relies on location, context, and circumstance. Also called contextual or spatial memory, it draws on the reality that we are always somewhere when we learn something. The context becomes a part of the memory and helps us to remember. Unlike semantic memory, episodic memory does not easily fail us. "Our episodic memory process has unlimited capacity, forms quickly, is easily updated, requires no practice, is effortless, and is used naturally by everyone."[25] Have you ever tried to recall something you read? Oftentimes, you can remember the location of the material on the page of the book but cannot bring the actual words to mind. This is episodic memory at work even as semantic memory fails us.

Taking seriously episodic memory in our teaching calls us to pay attention to the contexts within which we teach. The content of a teaching space is often what is called "invisible information" and becomes a part of the memory, providing another hook to aid in remembering. Designing bulletin boards with pictures related to a particular passage being studied, paying attention to the room arrangement and how students move and work in it, engaging as many senses as possible when teaching (i.e., having things to taste, touch, smell, and see)—all this becomes a part of episodic memory and provides pathways to recalling important information and learning.

Procedural memory is often called muscle memory. "Procedural memory stores memories of the processes that the body does."[26] Also called body learning, this memory type draws on actions and behaviors. Because the brain recognizes both the body and brain as part of the same connected organism, it is obvious from the brain's perspective that what happens to the body happens to the brain. This means that procedural memory is easily stored and easily recalled.

The presence of this type of memory offers important insight into how we approach teaching the Bible. As students will often tell you, their most memorable learning experiences were those based on "hands-on" or "whole body" learning. Karen recalls a teaching moment with the story of the bent-over woman in Luke 13:10–17. While working with this passage with a group of adults, she asked them to spend a few minutes in pairs, walking around the room. One member of the pair was to walk bent over while attempting to carry on a conversation. At a point, they were to switch roles and continue the conversation. For many weeks after that experience, those adults continued to talk about that lesson and the insights they gained from the experience of being bent over. Their procedural memory had been engaged, and their ability to remember and to deepen the meaning of the text for their lives was enhanced. Role-playing and dramatizing a biblical story are important techniques for engaging procedural memory.

Automatic memory is also referred to as conditioned response memory or reflexive memory. A great deal of what we recall is automatic. This is information that has instant associations for us and is recalled by just a word, a musical note, or a gesture. Multiplication tables and the alphabet are stored in automatic memory. Sets of words such as hot and cold, up and down, in and out, and stop and go, words where the naming of one automatically evokes the other, are stored here. Gestures such as shaking hands, where one person reaches out a hand and the other automatically reaches in return, are kept in automatic memory.

Information is placed in automatic memory by constant repetition and memorization. As a child, we learn to say the Lord's Prayer by hearing it prayed regularly in worship and repeating it over and over again. As adults, when we hear the words "Our Father," we hardly have to think before knowing what to say next. For many of our participants in the workshop described earlier, Psalm 23 was stored in automatic memory. All we had to do was say "The Lord is my shepherd" and voices joined in, knowing exactly what came next.

Although repetition and memorization are often criticized as boring techniques, there is clearly a role for such methods in our teaching. The key here is that they do not have to be boring. It wasn't boring to say the Lord's Prayer each Sunday as a part of worship, yet we were forming memory by its regular repetition. Songs are easily stored in automatic memory, so music is a natural way to rehearse and store information. The youth we know often have an amazing repertoire of songs by their favorite artists that they know by heart. Using that same passion for music as a teaching resource in the church in order to create automatic memory is important.

Certainly there is more to learning than storing information in automatic memory, but having some of the biblical stories and material readily at hand through this memory type enhances our efforts as teachers to help students build deeper and more meaningful connections with these stories and materials. Automatic memory also often activates the other memory types. As Sprenger says, "Your automatic memory may cause other memory lanes to open."[27] We saw this happening with our workshop participants. As they begin to repeat the words of Psalm 23, other memories and meanings related to the psalm emerged. Participants were able to recall where they first heard it, feelings connected with it, and meanings they had formed regarding it. Automatic memory is neither formed in isolation from other memory types nor accessed separately from them. Helping people increase their automatic memory becomes an important resource for accessing the multiple memories that make up meaningful learning.

The final memory type we want to discuss is *emotional memory*. This memory type is significant because it is the most powerful kind of memory. Sprenger describes this well:

> *Emotional memory takes precedence over any other kind of memory.* The brain always gives priority to emotions. When information enters the brain and reaches the thalamus, the amygdala will grab that information if it is emotional and go straight to work on it. If the information calls for strong emotion, especially fear, the amygdala takes over to prepare the body. Daniel Goleman…calls this response a "neural hijacking." At this point, no other memory lanes have a chance.[28]

Because emotions are so central to the brain's processing of information, this memory type plays a significant role in all that we learn. All information and experience has an emotional tone to it, whether it is pain or pleasure, challenge or threat, calm or passionate. Attending to the importance of emotion is key for those of us who teach in the church. As we said earlier, good teaching does not avoid emotions; it embraces them.

It is the strength of the emotional charge that is central to the brain's processing and determining what is stored in long-term memory. As teachers, we need to pay attention to this. A key question to ask is, What is emotionally significant about this information or experience for my students? Another way to ask the question is, What stake do the students have in this that they will want to remember it? We need to provide emotional hooks for the material we teach.

We were providing an emotional hook in our use of the McFerrin song with our workshop participants. We knew from experience that hearing the song would evoke some strong emotional responses. We also knew that sharing the context out of which the song came—a tribute to his mother—would provide additional emotional significance regarding why this might matter for our students. Through it all, we were certain that brains would be attentive and seeking to make connections and deepen meanings with regard to this psalm. From our perspective, such is our hope as teachers of the Bible!

To summarize, understanding memory and how it is formed is critical to our work as teachers. It enables us to realize that memory is more a process than a place, and we can teach in ways that assist the process of making memories and remembering. A key factor here is knowing something about the different types of memory and the role they play in our learning. Equally important is the knowledge that the more memory types we engage in our teaching, the richer the learning and the greater the chance that our students will be able to recall and remember. It is much easier to find information that has several pathways leading to it!

These insights shaped how we worked with Psalm 23 with our workshop participants. We drew on semantic and automatic memory when inviting them to recall the words of the psalm. We expanded the memory base by asking them to recall where they first heard it, where they had encountered this text, any images and feelings the text evoked, and so on, thus engaging episodic and emotional memory. We were aware of the possible emotional charge that the McFerrin rendition carried and trusted that this would grab and hold our participants' attention. Our hope was for the formation of new memories and the deepening of old memories, thereby expanding our participants' knowledge of Psalm 23 and the ability to access this knowledge in meaningful ways.

Learning Styles and Multiple Intelligences

Our discussion of how we learn would be incomplete without a brief consideration of learning styles and multiple intelligences. The importance of attending to these issues of learning is illustrated by the following. In her novel *A Woman's Place,* Marita Golden tells the story of three women and their efforts to claim their own identities. At one point, one of the women, Faith, talks about her struggles in college. She voices her frustration this way: "I just wish there was more than one way to learn what it is they want us to know. But it's all got to come out of a book and it's all got to be given back on a piece of paper."[29] Faith was confronting the pervasive misconception that we all learn the same way. The truth is that there are multiple ways in which we engage in the process of learning. As teachers of the Bible, we need to be sensitive to this and have some understanding of the various ways our students approach learning.

Learning Styles

The learning process is shaped by two basic factors: (1) how we *perceive,* become aware of, and receive data, information, and experience from the world around us; and (2) how we *process* that data and information, work with it, and integrate it into meaningful knowledge. The significant issue for those of us who teach is that different people have different ways in which they work at perceiving and processing. Each of us has our own unique *learning style,* that consistent pattern of behaviors by which we perceive and process data and experience from the world around us and make meaning of it. Several factors influence our learning style; among them our particular biological heritage, our personality, our unique life experiences, and the demands that a given learning situation places on us. However they are formed, we each have a preferred approach or style of learning.

There are various ways to talk about learning styles.[30] One of the things we have sought to avoid, however, is the creation of a fixed approach to styles that becomes a box into which we place people. There is no single right way to describe and categorize learning styles. The approach we have found helpful in working with our students and with teachers in the church is to reflect both on ways data can be perceived and also on options for processing our experience, knowing that each of us will have our own unique ways of doing and combining each of these.

Any discussion of how we perceive takes us to our five senses, the loading docks for our brains. Our senses are primary channels through which we take in information and experience the world around us. Research has shown that, as individuals, we have preferred sensory channels that we use. One of the helpful ways of framing these sensory channels comes from the work of Waynne James and Michael Galbraith.[31] They researched groups of students to see how they approached learning and what sensory channels they preferred to use. They discovered that the students they studied tended to group themselves into certain categories, which James and

Galbraith named "perceptual learning styles." They named seven such styles:

1. Visual: People who prefer sight or visual sense tend to learn through observation. They need visual stimuli such as pictures, charts, graphs, tables, and demonstrations they can watch. As Bible students they need to see maps and pictures instead of hearing descriptions of a given place.

2. Print: James and Galbraith discovered a distinction in those who preferred their visual channel. Some people seem to learn best through seeing the visual symbols we call words printed on a page. These folks are very word oriented and learn best through reading and writing, working with printed words. They easily retain information that they read, and as Bible students they need to see and read the text themselves.

3. Aural: People who prefer hearing, or engaging the aural channel, learn best through listening. They easily retain that which is presented verbally. Some people actually like listening to lectures and find it is easier to remember something they hear than something they read. As Bible students these folks need to hear the text read aloud.

4. Interactive: Similar to the visual and print distinction in the first two categories, James and Galbraith's research discovered a perceptual learning style category in which the person needs to verbalize out loud and to do so in the company of others. These people need to talk things out and discuss them. More than just a listening experience, something in the interaction helps them to learn. These Bible students find small-group discussions to be very beneficial.

5. Haptic: Some individuals perceive their world best through their sense of touch. A haptic learner is someone who has to feel, touch, and handle objects. They can't just listen and watch; they have to touch. Often these people need to be touching others as they are talking with them. As Bible students they need as much hands-on experience as possible. Being able to touch and anoint with oil when hearing Psalm

23:5, "You anoint my head with oil," can be important to a haptic learner.

6. Olfactory: One of the interesting perceptual channels that James and Galbraith name is the olfactory channel. Some people seem to learn best through their senses of smell and taste. They can often vividly associate data and information with particular smells and tastes. When teaching these students the Bible, we want to pay close attention to the place of taste and smell in the text. Making use of actual frankincense and myrrh when teaching the story of the wise men (Matthew 2) can be significant for olfactory learners.

7. Kinesthetic: Among our students are those who learn best through movement, with their whole body engaged in the experience. Even if they have to sit and listen, kinesthetic learners often have some part of the body moving, whether it is a swinging foot or a hand doodling on paper. The exercise used with the story of the bent-over woman in Luke, described earlier in this chapter, is an example of engaging the kinesthetic learning style.

A significant point to remember is that people generally are not limited to just one of these as their preferred perceptual learning style, but tend to integrate two or more into their particular approach. The important issue is that people perceive data and information from the world around them in a variety of ways. As teachers of the Bible, it is vital that we be sensitive to this and find ways to help people learn that are engaging and helpful to their preferred styles.

Just as there are different ways people perceive the world around them, there are also different ways in which people process the information and experiences they have. To return briefly to the human brain, research has discovered at least two different and complementary ways in which the brain processes information. The first approach is associated with the left hemisphere of the brain. The left hemisphere tends to work with data and information in parts, recognizing the parts that make up a whole. It likes to take the data apart and lay things out in a linear and sequential pattern, working with it in a step-by-step fashion. It relies primarily on language as a processing tool and works with verbal information with great efficiency. Words such as "analytical" and "logical" are used to describe this way of processing. In Bible study a student with a preference for this processing approach will be drawn to working through a passage verse by verse, seeking to make sense of the parts before looking at the bigger picture.

The second approach is associated with the right hemisphere of the brain. This hemisphere likes to work with wholes and prefers synthesis. It is good at constructing patterns and relationships out of the data and experience perceived. It does not move linearly, but processes simultaneously, almost like the snap of a finger. It works most efficiently with visual and spatial information. Its language capacity is extremely limited, and words seem to play little or no part in its processing of information. Words such as "intuitive" and "spontaneous" are used to describe this way of processing. In Bible study a student with a preference for this processing approach will be interested in looking for patterns in a biblical text and exploring what those might mean. For example, a student with this preference would more likely notice the repetitions in a given text, such as "And God said...God saw that it was good...And there was evening and there was morning" in Genesis 1, and wonder about them. These students also will often intuit a meaning for a text, but have to struggle to put that into words. The use of artistic expression can be helpful to such students.

Although these different and complementary ways are associated with the different hemispheres of the brain, we need to remember it is the *whole* brain that learns! The human brain is a "parallel processor," meaning that it processes a lot of data simultaneously, even if it is doing this in different ways. The brain is always seeking to relate the data and connect things. At its core the brain seeks connection.

Even while the whole brain is learning, however, we tend to have a preference for one of the ways of processing just described. Some of us work better when things are presented in a logical, analytical, sequential manner. Others absorb simultaneous images, making sense out of them quickly. They see patterns and intuit meanings even when they cannot verbalize them. What is important to remember here is that the brain engages both forms of processing, and we risk inhibiting learning when we overlook either process in our teaching of the Bible.

In addition to the ways in which the brain processes information are different behaviors we engage when we are working to make sense and meaning out of information we receive. David Kolb, in his research on learning styles,[32] identifies two primary behaviors. The first of these is *reflection*. Some people process information and experience through reflection and observation. These are the students who tend to sit back and observe, reflect, think about what is going on. They are often initially quiet in discussions and can appear on the surface to be unengaged. But their inner dialogue is usually quite active. They are busy processing through inner reflection and observation.

Others, however, immediately engage in action with regard to the information they perceive. Kolb calls this behavior "active experimentation." These are the people who have their hands up to answer a question before any one else, who quickly begin to talk in a discussion, who are the first out of their chairs to take part in an activity, who will begin taking a test before reading all the directions or instructions. These people process their learning through *action* and *doing*.

As teachers of the Bible, we need to pay attention to these different ways with our students. Some people will be logical and linear in their approach, drawing easily on words to express their thoughts. Others will be more intuitive and spontaneous, not as quick to find verbal expression for what they are thinking. We will also see both reflection and action used as behaviors for processing experiences. Our challenge as teachers is to teach in ways that engage the whole person, that draw on all these ways of processing. We will then be assisting our students to learn in ways that are appropriate and useful to them.

In our desire to teach in ways that help others to learn, there is one important fact we must keep in mind. *Our tendency as teachers is to teach to our own learning style.* For example, a visual learner will want to use lots of pictures, diagrams, and other visual stimuli in her teaching. It is as natural as breathing air. After all, this is the way we learn, and we assume that others learn the same way. The challenge we face as teachers is to expand our own approaches to learning, to explore other ways of perceiving and processing, and to develop a greater sensitivity to the different ways our students learn and the ability to assist that learning in helpful ways.

Multiple Intelligences [33]

Not to be confused with learning styles, the theory of multiple intelligences also provides helpful insights for those of us called to teach in the church. In fact, this theory is the conceptual framework behind a new approach to education and teaching the Bible that is gaining wide acceptance in the church today: the workshop rotation model.[34]

In the early 1980s, Dr. Howard Gardner, professor of education at Harvard, challenged the view that intelligence is a singular property, something we each possess that is fixed and unchangeable and that we each have in different "amounts." This old view measured intelligence via an "intelligence quotient," IQ, and a higher IQ supposedly meant we possessed more of this thing called intelligence and therefore were "smarter." Gardner developed a theory that looked at intelligence in a totally different way; it became known as the multiple intelligences theory.

In the simplest terms, Gardner defines intelligence as *the human potential or capacity to know and to solve problems*. Rather than being a quantity of something, intelligence is the *capacity* to *process* information. The concept of multiple intelligences grew out of Gardner's belief and observations that there are various ways in which we as human beings come to know something and that learning involves the engagement of a variety of these capacities we possess. It is our belief that we need to learn to value and to draw on these multiple intelligences in our work as teachers of the Bible in the church.

Before briefly discussing each of the intelligences and how they might shape our work as teachers of the Bible, we want to make some general observations. First, Gardner calls these intelligences "bio-psychological potentials." In other words, intelligences are shaped by both nature and nurture. Each of us has these potentials, even though certain factors may limit their development (e.g., biology, injury, culture, experiences, etc.). Second, all people are alike in that they have these intelligences. We may differ in the strengths of these capacities, but we all have them. Third, most people can develop each intelligence to an adequate level of competency. A nurturing environment is key here, because an intelligence needs to be used in order to develop. Fourth, intelligences usually work together in rich and complex ways. For example, a pianist not only uses musical intelligence to perform in concert, she also employs interpersonal intelligence to communicate with the other musicians, intrapersonal intelligence to interpret the music, and kinesthetic intelligence to manipulate the piano keys. Our goal, therefore, is not to teach to a particular intelligence, but to teach in ways that engage them all. In doing so, our students' potential for learning is enhanced. Finally, there are many ways to "be intelligent" within each of the seven intelligences[35] described next. Our challenge as teachers is to value all of them in all their diversity.

The seven intelligences are:

1. *Linguistic Intelligence*
   This is our capacity as humans to speak, understand, read, and use words effectively, whether orally or in writing. Among the skills this intelligence uses are talking, writing, reading, and comprehending words. Sensitivity to the sounds, structure, meanings, and functions of words reflect a strength in this intelligence. People who are strongly linguistic think in words and love reading, writing, telling stories, playing word games, and so on. They are what we call "word smart."

   To help our students engage and develop this intelligence, we need to read about, write about, talk about, and listen to. This means that verbal presentations, books, writing activities, storytelling, journal writing, choral reading, and so on are important teaching methods for linguistic intelligence.

2. *Logical-Mathematical Intelligence*
   This intelligence draws attention to our capacity to know and figure out patterns of cause and effect and to reason well. It includes a sensitivity to logical patterns and relationships and the ability to handle long chains of reasoning. Among the skills used in this intelligence are categorization, classification,

inference, generalization, and hypothesis testing. People who are strongly logical-mathematical think by reasoning and love to experiment, question, calculate, figure out logical puzzles, and so on. They are what we might call "pattern smart." They easily see the pattern in something. Making sense of biblical material can call for skill in logic, integration, and inquiry, all strengths of this intelligence.

To teach to this intelligence, we need to quantify, conceptualize, and invite our students to think critically. Among the helpful teaching methods we can employ are classifying or categorizing subject matter, logical puzzles or games, experiments and demonstrations, Socratic questioning (the use of questions to help students explore their own thinking), and problem solving.

3. *Spatial Intelligence*
Spatial intelligence has to do with the capacity to see and know visual and spatial patterns, shades, colors, and connections. It includes the ability to perceive the visual-spatial world accurately and then to act on that world to transform it. This intelligence involves sensitivity to color, line, shape, form, and space and the relationships that exist between these elements. It can be seen in our ability to make and read a map, know where something is located, understand and identify shapes, recognize faces, and so on. People who are strongly spatial think in images and pictures and love to design, draw, visualize, sculpt, paint, build, and doodle. They are said to be "picture smart."

To teach to this intelligence, we need to provide opportunities for our students to see, draw, build, visualize, color, symbolize, and create mind maps. Charts, graphs, maps, diagrams, photography, painting, drawing, collages, art prints, illustrations, graphic symbols, and video become important teaching methods for working with this intelligence.

4. *Bodily-Kinesthetic Intelligence*
The capacity to understand and perform meaningful and functional movements with our bodies is the mark of the

bodily-kinesthetic intelligence. This intelligence includes the ability to use one's whole body to express ideas and feelings and the facility to use one's hands to produce or transform things. It is marked by skill in coordination, balance, dexterity, strength, flexibility, and speed and includes the ability to control one's body movements and handle objects skillfully. People who are strongly bodily-kinesthetic think via bodily sensations and love to dance, run, jump, build, touch, gesture, and so on.

To teach to this intelligence, we need to provide opportunities to act out, dance, build, and touch. Among the helpful teaching methods we can use are drama, mime, dance, creative movement, signing, crafts, role play, hands-on activities of all kinds, physical expression, and sculpting with clay. Teachers of the Bible who draw on gestures, postures, and dramatic re-creations of biblical stories are engaging this intelligence.

5. *Musical Intelligence*

This intelligence reveals our capacity to perceive, discriminate, transform, and express musical forms. It includes sensitivity to the rhythm, pitch or melody, and timbre or tone color of a musical piece. It is seen in the ability to appreciate various forms of musical expression. It involves skills in singing, playing a musical instrument, writing music, voice inflection, and enjoying and understanding music. People who are strongly musical are good at reflecting via rhythms and melodies and love to sing, hum, whistle, tap feet and hands, and listen to music. It can be said that they are "music smart."

To teach to this intelligence, we need to include singing, signing, rapping, and playing and listening to music in our Bible studies. Methods we can use include singing hymns, playing musical instruments, creating songs, listening to recordings, providing background music, and choral reading.

6. *Interpersonal Intelligence*

This intelligence draws attention to our capacity to perceive and respond appropriately to the moods, temperaments, intentions, motivations, feelings, and desires of other people. It includes a sensitivity to facial expressions, voice, and gestures; the capacity for discriminating among many different kinds of interpersonal cues; and the ability to respond effectively to those cues in some pragmatic way. Interpersonal intelligence provides us with the ability to "read" other people and helps us to live in relationship and community with others. People who are strong in this intelligence reflect best by bouncing ideas off other people and love to relate, organize, mediate, and work with others. They can be called "people smart."

To teach to this intelligence, we need to discuss, collaborate, and interact. Appropriate teaching methods include cooperative group activities, simulations, group brainstorming, group planning, conversation, and role play. This intelligence invites those of us who teach the Bible to take seriously the communal nature of such work.

7. *Intrapersonal Intelligence*
   According to Gardner, we each have an intelligence about what is going on in our own psyche and spirit, and this is called intrapersonal intelligence. This capacity includes the ability to know ourselves and to act and adapt on the basis of that knowledge. It involves having an accurate picture of oneself, including one's strengths and limitations; an awareness of inner moods, intentions, motivations, temperaments, and desires; and the capacity for self-discipline, self-understanding, and self-esteem. People who are strong in this intelligence reflect from deep inside themselves and are good at meditating, dreaming, spending time in silence, and setting personal goals. They are known as "self smart."

   To teach to this intelligence, we need to offer opportunities for individual reflection in order for people to think about and to connect the biblical text to one's personal life. Useful teaching methods include guided meditation, silence, journal keeping, exercises that bring feelings into the study, and experiences that invite students to consider how to apply insights to their personal lives.

Awareness of multiple intelligences, like awareness of learning styles, enables us as teachers to be sensitive to the variety of ways in which our students learn. Such knowledge makes it possible for us to teach in a manner that will engage these various styles and intelligences and thereby help our students to learn in ways that work best for them. Research has shown that students learn best when they are excited and engaged. They are more likely to be both excited and engaged when they are learning in ways that best fit their particular abilities and skills. If we want our students to develop a passion for and draw meaning from the Bible, then teaching in ways that address the various learning styles and multiple intelligences present in our students, in ways that excite and engage them, seems a worthy challenge and goal!

Summary and Implications for Teaching the Bible

How people learn is vital information for teachers of the Bible. Understanding how our brain works and how memory is formed, knowing the different ways in which we each perceive and process information and experience and therefore the different styles of learning present in our students, and recognizing the different intelligences at work in our educational settings—all this can help us teach in ways that captivate and stimulate our students. It seems important, then, in closing, to consider the implications of all this for teaching the Bible. What significant insights might we name? Although certainly not exhaustive of the possible insights, we want to name six key principles that have emerged out of this knowledge for our own teaching and challenge our readers to consider these principles in the shaping of their own teaching.

1. *Teach to and for connection.* Remember that the brain is a natural connecting organ and searches for the connections between the various data and information it receives. We can teach for connection by exploring what our students already know about a subject, by organizing our material and creating brain "maps" that help students see connections in what we are teaching, and by drawing on our students' own life experiences for illustrations, thus helping them see the connection between the Bible and their everyday living.

2. *Remember that emotions are critical to learning.* Emotion drives attention, and attention is critical to learning and remembering.

Information needs to have an "emotional charge" in order for the brain to select it for long-term memory. When teaching, we must pay attention to our students' feelings about a subject, regularly asking the question, In what way can I help this topic really matter to them? It is important to look for and help to create emotional significance for the texts we teach.

3. *Teach to challenge, not to threaten.* In our teaching it is important to take seriously the brain's natural impulse to protect us from threat. Remember that the brain's movement in moments of threat is toward survival, a kind of reflexive, downshifting into automatic responses designed to take care of us. However, the brain is also drawn to challenge and is stimulated by it. Therefore, we need to be sensitive to the line between challenge and threat in our students. We teach to challenge by providing new and novel ways of thinking and doing, by offering a range of sensory stimulation that engages all five of the senses, by offering choices so the brain must decide, and by providing as enriched an environment for learning as possible. We teach to avoid threat by creating safe space where students feel free to be themselves, to question, to explore, and by providing freedom for students to express doubts and struggles, to share their stories, knowing they will be treated with respect and care.

4. *Remember that all learning begins with sensory experiences.* Our five senses are the primary "loading docks" through which the brain receives data and information. The more senses involved, the richer the possible connections with a given experience. Therefore, we need to teach through seeing, hearing, touching, tasting, and smelling, engaging all five senses in the learning experience.

5. *Teach to a variety of learning styles and intelligences.* A learning style is the particular pattern of behaviors by which a person perceives and processes data and experience from the world around him or her. People do this perceiving and processing in different ways and therefore have different learning styles. In order to honor these different styles, our teaching needs to include visual, aural, kinesthetic, haptic, olfactory, and interactive experiences. Encouraging analysis and intuition, logic and spontaneity, and linear and simultaneous thinking is important. Providing time for reflection *and* active experimentation is vital. Engaging the multiple intelligences present in any given teaching context is critical.

6. Remember these key words: Rehearse, Reflect, and Connect. The brain learns best when it can *rehearse* information and data over and over again. We need to repeat the Bible stories we teach, to visit them several different times in different ways. The brain needs to *reflect* on the information and data it receives. It needs time to think about what it is learning, so guarding against trying to cover too much at a time is important. Allow time for students to reflect and think, and they will be more apt to remember what they have learned. Finally, as our first principle already stated, the brain needs to *connect* the new information with what students already know and what they have learned before. Always teach for connection!

2

Teaching the Bible: How We Teach

Mrs. H., Mrs. K., Dr. L., Dr. M., Miss Evelyn—we all can name them. They are those teachers who shaped and influenced our lives in meaningful ways, even though we cannot always define and describe how in a precise manner. We only know that when asked to think of a significant teacher in our lives, these people come to mind. Not all of them are professional teachers. Some of them are volunteers—Sunday school teachers, vacation Bible school teachers, youth camp teachers—people who had a passion for learning and wanted to share that passion with others. Whether professional or volunteer, they all taught us in profound and important ways. These were teachers of the Bible who helped to open the pages of this ancient and authoritative text for us.

How did they do that? How did they teach in ways that helped us to learn, that engaged and empowered us to know? The answers to these questions are as varied as the teachers we could each name. Just as people learn in many different ways, teachers teach in many different ways. Our purpose in this chapter is not to tell our readers the one right way to go about teaching, because we do not believe that there is one right way to teach. Instead, our goal in this chapter is to engage in some reflection regarding the activity of teaching, what it is, and what we need to know about being a teacher that can assist us to be one who makes a difference.

The place we often begin this reflection with our students is to invite them to think about a teacher of the Bible they have had who had a significant impact on their lives and their knowledge of scripture, someone they would identify as a good teacher. Across several years of doing this, we have been introduced to a wide range of teachers with different personalities, abilities, and skills and representing a broad spectrum of models of teaching. Our observation is that no two of these teachers we've met through our students have been exactly alike.

However, in dialogue with the students, we discovered some commonality in the teachers they described. This commonality begins with a definition of teaching they all seemed to embody. We define teaching as *the process of making accessible experience and knowledge in ways that assist people to make sense and meaning of it for their own lives.* Each of the teachers the students named seemed to have a knack for "making accessible" what the students needed to know and in the way they needed to know it. In pressing further at this ability to make accessible, we explored what it was about these teachers that seemed to enable them to do this. Again, we found a lot of unique qualities about the teachers described. But we also saw some points of commonality, some "knowledges" these teachers seemed to possess that facilitated their teaching efforts.

We use the term *knowledges* to represent a broader perspective than just a collection of facts and information. *Knowledges* points to ways of knowing that go beyond the concrete and factual. Some of the knowledge good teachers possess is intuitive, a kind of knowing that they can't define in precise terms but that is nonetheless true. Such knowing reminds us that teaching is as much an art as it is a science and can't be limited to knowing and using the right techniques and methods.

The kinds of knowing we kept hearing described in our students' portraits of significant teachers began to group themselves into certain categories. We discovered six categories of teacher knowledges that we believe are worthy of note: (1) knowledge of self, (2) knowledge of students, (3) knowledge of content, (4) knowledge of space, (5) knowledge of teaching models, and (6) knowledge of methods and techniques. Although we do not claim that these are the only knowledges teachers have or need, we do believe that these represent some of the key qualities of good teachers. Let us now turn our attention to each of these knowledges and what they have to tell us about how we teach.

Knowledge of Self

Good teachers possess a knowledge of who they are and the ways in which this shapes what they do and why they do it. Parker Palmer, in his excellent work *The Courage to Teach,* makes this important statement: "We teach who we are."[1] He goes on to say that "good teaching requires self-knowledge"[2] and that "good teaching cannot be reduced to technique; good teaching comes from the identity and integrity of the teacher."[3] As we often say to our students, techniques do not teach, *people* do. We can only truly think about "how" to teach in the context of "who" is teaching. In talking about teaching the Bible in the church, the person of the teacher and the act of teaching go hand in hand. As one church school teacher put it, "One of the major things you do as a Sunday school teacher is you share yourself, you know, with the children and some of your perspectives on life and situations and that kind of thing."[4] We do, indeed, teach ourselves.

If we teach ourselves and therefore knowledge of self is vital for a teacher, what do we need to know about ourselves as teachers? Knowing one's self is a lifelong work, so we do not believe that to be a teacher of the Bible one has to have it "all figured out." Mystery is an important part of what it means to be human, too. But there are some things about ourselves that are helpful to know in order to teach the Bible in ways beneficial to our students. These include our motivations for teaching, the personal and cultural perspectives that shape how we view the Bible, our own learning styles, and the gifts we bring to teaching.

What motivates you to teach? Where are your passions with regard to students and content? These are important questions that a teacher of the Bible needs to ask. Our reason for raising these questions is not to claim that there are certain motives that are better than others. We teach for a variety of reasons. But we do believe that good teachers have a conscious awareness of what motivates them to teach.

In her research on church school teachers, Karen found a wide range of motives present in the teachers she interviewed.[5] What concerned her was that many of these were unexamined motives. By raising the issue of motives, our hope is that teachers will examine and bring to consciousness the reasons they teach and why they teach the way they do. Knowing our motives offers us the option of choice, of choosing to continue doing what we are doing or changing in ways that might be helpful for our students.

A seminary student returning from a summer's internship in a local church shared the following encounter. She was teaching a Bible study for a group of college-age students. It was their first session together, and she was all excited about sharing the many new things she had learned about the Bible in her previous year's seminary classes. The topic of this study was Ephesians, and she decided to begin the study with a discussion of the authorship of that book. She had been fascinated by such discussions in her own classes and thought others would be too. She brought several Bible commentaries to the class and immediately had the students begin to research questions of authorship. To her surprise, one of the students became quite vocal about her dislike of such research and wanted to know why they couldn't just read the Bible and see what it had to say. The teacher kept trying to explain how important it was to her to consider this question of authorship, but to no avail. That first session ended with the teacher wondering what had gone wrong and how she might deal with such a problem in the future.

One of the things this young teacher needed to examine was her motive for teaching. She was teaching in order to duplicate her own experience. Karen heard this same motive at work in some of the teachers she interviewed. They were teaching in order to help the children they taught have the same experiences with the Bible they had had. One teacher put it this way: "And the thing I enjoy most about teaching Sunday school is the Bible stories. 'Cause I can remember having people tell 'em to me when I was a child and I can bring back all those experiences and I really get into it."[6] Certainly we want to share the good news we have received, but in neither of these instances had the teachers paused to reflect on whether their particular experiences were appropriate for the students they now taught.

Teaching because we want to duplicate our own experiences and share our favorite Bible stories, or because "we've always done it this way," or because we want to impress our students with our knowledge and skill is teaching that is probably not grounded in the most helpful of motives. As an ancient Hebrew proverb puts it, "Do not confine your children to your own learning for they were born in another time."[7] Teaching that truly helps us to make accessible the experience and knowledge our students need calls for a conscious reflection on our motives.

A teacher also needs to know something of his or her own personal and cultural perspectives and how these shape his or her teaching the Bible. Thomas Groome puts it this way: "We should be conscious of any biases, fears, vested interests, and closed-mindedness that we bring to interpret the texts of the tradition."[8] We all have biases and perspectives. There is simply no way to view the world or the Bible from a neutral stance. As with motives, the problem arises when we lack awareness of those biases and perspectives, when we cannot name them and see how they might influence the way we read a text. It is this lack of awareness that limits our ability to choose ways to read and interpret biblical texts that would be helpful and appropriate for our students and would assist in making the Bible more accessible to them. We will be exploring issues related to cultural perspectives and biases and the various ways in which we can "read" or interpret texts in the next chapters. For now the important point we want to make is the way a lack of awareness limits us.

One of the teachers Karen interviewed talked about her view of the Bible in this way:

> The Bible is not just something that's read, snatches of it are read on Sunday morning…It's a story book of real people's lives. You know, that there is a history there of real people who live as we do and eat and breathe and have friends and family and troubles and also have a belief and that's the core of something that's come down through time. Ah, to get that idea of a history and the fact that the children are a part of history—part of a line coming down through time and that it will go on after us.[9]

It is clear from this teacher's comments that she reads the Bible as a history book and has a great deal of passion for that perspective. Although both of us applaud this teacher's passion, and neither of us would argue that there is a historical nature to scripture, to read the Bible in the same way one would read a history of the American frontier runs the risk of misconstruing the nature and purpose of the biblical text. An awareness on the part of this teacher regarding the perspective she brings to her work affords her the opportunity to reflect on how she reads and to consider other options that may prove helpful and appropriate with her students. Such knowledge of self is vital for the teaching task.

Another knowledge of self that a teacher needs is knowledge of his or her learning style. We've already said a great deal about learning styles in chapter 1 and do not need to repeat that material here. But we would be remiss in this discussion about how to teach if we did not remind our readers that knowing one's own particular approach to learning is important. Our tendency is to teach in ways that are compatible with our own particular learning style. We just assume that because this is the way we learn best, it must be the best way for others too. As teachers of the Bible, we need both an awareness of how we learn and an awareness of other approaches to learning. With such knowledge, we are then able to expand our teaching repertoire to include methods and experiences that speak to the wide variety of learning styles present in our students.

A final knowledge of self is knowing the gifts we bring to teaching. Often when people hear the word *gifts,* they think of talents and skills. Of course it is helpful if we know what unique talents and skills we bring to our work as teachers. Some teachers have a knack for preparing and delivering good lectures. Others are particularly skilled in leading discussions. Some are good storytellers. All these are important skills for teachers of the Bible.

However, when we talk about knowing what gifts we bring to teaching, we are not talking about talents and skills. We are talking about the unique qualities of being that we each bring to this important ministry of teaching the Bible. Parker Palmer talks about this as the "heart" of a teacher, "meaning *heart* in its ancient sense, as the place where intellect and emotion and spirit and will converge in the human self."[10] What are the qualities of our heart, of our very being, that are marks of a "good" teacher?

Palmer says that good teachers "possess a capacity for connectedness."[11] They are able to weave connections among themselves, their students, and the subject matter that make a difference in students' lives. In the stories of teachers our students have shared, we've heard other important qualities of "heart" mentioned. These include courage and the willingness to try new ways of expression; commitment and the ability to be what Jerry Larsen calls an "eyewitness,"[12] giving witness to the impact of the biblical story in one's own life; a sense of humility and a willingness to be vulnerable, to admit when one doesn't know; and an openness to one's own continued growth in faith. These qualities and more represent the gifts we bring to the work of teaching the Bible.

Good teachers know who they are and who they aren't. They know something of what motivates them; they can name some of the biases and perspectives that shape their view of scripture; they understand how they best learn and also how others might learn differently; and they can name and claim the gifts they bring to the teaching task. Although certainly not exhaustive of all we might know about ourselves as teachers, these "knowledges of self" are vital and important to the ministry of teaching the Bible.

Knowledge of Students

"The students we teach are larger than life and even more complex. To see them clearly and see them whole, and respond to them wisely in the moment, requires a fusion of Freud and Solomon that few of us achieve."[13] As Parker Palmer so wisely reminds us, we cannot know all there is to know about the people we teach. Yet some knowledge of those we teach, such as who they are and what we need to know about them, is vital for teachers of the Bible.

What are some of the important things we need to know about people in order to teach in ways that "make accessible"? We've already talked in chapter 1 in some detail about one of the things we need to know, and that is how people learn. In addition to this important information, there are other areas of understanding that can be of benefit as we seek to teach faithfully. These include (1) biological, psychological, and cultural natures of our students, and (2) cognitive development and its role in human learning.

Biological, Psychological, and Cultural Natures of Humans

People come in all sizes and shapes. A few moments observing shoppers in a local mall will make one quite aware of this fact! It is important as teachers of the Bible that we remember that our students are complex and multidimensional and that one size does not fit all. Even though persons come in all sizes and shapes—or in the unique and particular, as we often say to our students—some aspects of being human have significant influence on how we teach. These include the biological, psychological, and cultural nature of persons.

It is important to remember that our students are biological beings. They are living organisms shaped and formed in certain ways. They come in a particular sex (and there *are* differences between males and females); they have certain physical abilities and limitations; they are a certain number of years old; and they are physically maturing and changing in certain ways. Because of our biological development, we are able to perform different tasks at different times in our lives. For example, small children do not have highly developed fine motor skills. Asking them as a part of a Bible study to do a craft exercise that requires lots of small movements and manipulations with their fingers is often an exercise in frustration for them. However, engaging them in whole body movements, such as acting out a Bible story, is much more compatible with their biological development.

A sensitivity to the biological nature of our students helps us to be attentive to the needs of our older students too. Both of us have taught classes of older adults in local churches and are sensitive to the need to regularly check to see if the class participants can hear what is being said and can see the chalkboard or easel on which we are writing. Making copies of handouts with larger print has proved helpful on several occasions. Research shows that both sight and hearing decline with age, and to ignore this prevents our older students from engaging fully in the learning process.

Biological factors affect learning in myriad ways. To illustrate, there have been several recent news reports regarding the research on adolescents that suggests they are not getting enough sleep. But there may be other factors at work besides staying up too late and trying to cram too much into a day. Brain research is suggesting that adolescents may actually function on an internal time clock that is different from adults.[14] When most adults are waking up and getting ready to go to work, teenagers are just getting down to serious sleep. The lack of youth energy for a Sunday morning Bible study class may have as much to do with biology as it does with interest and motivation. Understanding more about how the adolescent brain works and sleeps can be a great help in knowing when our youth are paying attention and learning and when they are likely to be nodding off.

In addition to being biological beings, we are also psychological beings. We have different personalities and relate in different ways to the world and to one another. Among the students we have taught both in the seminary and in the church, we have noted a wide range of responses and behaviors to class experiences. We have observed students who are the quiet ones, who don't speak a lot, who like to sit back and reflect on what is happening and what they are hearing. Others, however, are just the opposite. They are quite talkative, have their hands up almost before a question is asked, and tend to dominate class discussions, sometimes whether they have something to say or not!

There is nothing wrong with any of these students; they are just different and relate to and respond to the world in different ways. As teachers it is our task to attend to each of these and make sure they are included in the learning process. We need to allow time for reflection for the quiet students and make room for them when they want to enter the discussion. Sometimes it is hard for them to speak out among their more outspoken peers. A helpful technique is to use small groups of three or four for some discussions. This provides room for the quiet ones to talk.

We also need to provide ample time for discussion for the more talkative students so they can do the reflecting out loud that is helpful to their learning process. Sometimes our work with these students is to help them focus their thoughts and responses. They can be so busy talking that they do not hear what they are saying. We also need to help each of these students appreciate the other and what they bring to the conversation. Attending to the psychological nature of our students is an important responsibility for a teacher of the Bible.

In addition to their biological and psychological natures, our students are also cultural beings. Who we are as persons is shaped by our families and communities, the environments within which we grow and develop, and the life situations within which we live. We acquire certain manners and traditions, certain values that tell us how to live and relate in the world. We learn particular ways of behaving, of interacting, even of seeing the world. and we bring these cultural perspectives to our study of the Bible.

Although we will say a great deal more in a later chapter about the cultural issues related to teaching the Bible, we want to alert our readers at this point to the influence that culture has on our students. We all have our taken-for-granted ways of seeing and being in the world. Like reaching out a hand to shake when welcoming another, we often do not even think of the cultural rules that shape our lives. And this is true of our approach to the Bible. We have seen students who have learned such a reverence for the Bible in their cultural contexts that it is a struggle for them to question and engage in a critical study of the text. It was simply unheard of to question scripture in their cultural setting. Being aware of the cultural perspectives our students bring is one of the important tasks in teaching the Bible.

Cognitive Development

It is important to remember that our students are cognitive beings. In other words, they are capable of knowing and constructing knowledge. However, these capabilities develop in different ways at different points in the life cycle. It is especially important for teachers of children to understand something of the cognitive abilities of the children with whom they work.

Jean Piaget, a Swiss psychologist, has been particularly helpful to us in thinking about how children will hear and process the Bible stories they study. Piaget was interested in cognitive development and came to his theory through careful observations of children as they grew and changed across their childhood years. He named four primary stages of cognitive development: (1) sensorimotor stage (birth to 2 years), (2) preoperational stage (2 to 7 years), (3) concrete operational stage (7 to 11 years), and (4) formal operations stage (11 to 14 years).[15] Please note that the ages listed are approximate. Each person is unique and moves through the developmental process at his or her own particular pace.

Piaget observed that our mental abilities evolve and expand across time from birth into our adolescent years and beyond. Infants or toddlers in the sensorimotor period have limited abilities through which to engage the world. They can recognize themselves as objects distinct from other objects in their environment, and they have awareness of their immediate space and some sense of time. But their ability to engage in representational thought—for example, to know that the word *cat* represents a certain animal—and to use language to express themselves is rather limited. To try to "teach" Bible stories to this age group is not a helpful activity. The most important thing we can do for these very young children in the church is to help them know they are loved and that this community of people can be trusted. We can begin to share simple verses about God's love and faithfulness, trusting that they will sense that this book we read is important and that we are providing the foundation for more fruitful engagement with the Bible in the future.

The preoperational child has expanded mental abilities and widens the use of representational thought. Language development continues, and the child can now speak in fairly complex sentences. It is important to remember, however, that children in this stage have difficulty differentiating among truth, fantasy, and realism. In addition, their concept of space and time, though expanded over the sensorimotor stage, is still limited. Past, present, and future are confined to a short period. To talk about Jesus living two thousand years ago holds little real meaning for children in this stage. To try to teach a biblical concept such as grace or salvation to a child this age is not particularly useful. One of the best things we can do with preoperational children is to share with them some of the biblical stories and avoid trying to make a point or saying, "The meaning of this story is…"

We need to choose those stories carefully, though. Many can be quite frightening to children, such as the sacrifice of Isaac told in Genesis 22. A teacher of the Bible to children needs to always ask, What will the children hear in this? How will they interpret it? Young children can hear a statement such as "I have Jesus in my heart" and wonder, How did he get inside of me? Did I swallow him? We need to think carefully about how preoperational children will hear the story.

When teachers of young children take seriously the boundaries of preoperational thought, they sometimes find themselves struggling with what it means to "teach," especially if teaching has meant the imparting of facts and information and making sure the children get it "right." It is then important to remember that at this stage we are continuing to build a foundation of love and respect for the Bible, not making sure they get it "right." This foundation of love, respect, and curiosity will provide a solid basis on which to build as our children grow and develop.

The concrete operational child has become a logical thinker and can do reversible or cause-and-effect thinking. The child can perform a lot of what Piaget calls "mental operations," including reasoning, being aware of variables in a situation, and understanding the relationship between parts and whole. These children can begin to hear the Bible stories not just as individual stories but as part of a bigger story—the story of God and God's people. They have a sense of history lacking in the previous stages. But it is important to realize that children in this stage, particularly during the early part of it, still tend to be literalists. They think concretely, and it is easy for them to read the Bible as a factual history book, becoming frustrated if the facts don't agree.

In the formal operations stage, young adolescents develop the ability to do conceptual thinking. They are able to imagine other possibilities, create theories, think of time and explain infinity, and think symbolically. If we have done our work well as teachers of the Bible in the earlier stages of cognitive development, we will discover young people at this age able to engage in serious and thoughtful Bible study that will help them draw meaning for their own lives from the text.

Knowledge of students is critical for a teacher. Understanding who they are—knowing something of their biological, psychological, cultural, and cognitive makeup—will enable us to teach in ways that "make accessible" and assist our students in the important task of learning and making meaning of the biblical story for their own lives.

Knowledge of Content

"The subjects we teach are as large and complex as life, so our knowledge of them is always flawed and partial."[16] Although it goes without saying that knowing the content we teach is vital, Palmer reminds us of the humility with which we need to approach this knowledge. It is impossible to know everything, nor are we expected to. One of the comments we often hear from teachers regarding the reason why they enjoy teaching is how much they themselves are learning in the process. Our knowledge of content, therefore, is always a work in progress, and hopefully our own learning with regard to the Bible is ongoing.

Realizing that it is impossible to know everything, it is helpful, however, to give some thought and consideration to the content we want our students to encounter. It seems to us that there are two important questions of content we need to ask: (1) *What* do we want our students to know? and (2) *How* do we want them to know it?

The answer to the first question seems pretty obvious. We want our students to know the Bible, to know its stories, its history, its teachings, and so on. To do that, it is important that we as teachers know this too. This means we need to be committed to doing careful exegesis, or critical study, of the text. As we often say to our seminary students, we have to do our own homework with the text first. We cannot teach what we do not know, and the more in-depth we can know it, the more able we will be to engage our students in a careful and critical study of the text.

Such knowing of the text enables us to make decisions regarding the appropriateness of a given passage for the students we teach. It helps us think about how children might hear and interpret a given story, whether it is a suitable story for children of a certain age, and, if suitable, how best to teach it. It helps us think about the ways in which the adults we teach might hear the text and how we can then help them make meaningful and relevant connections.

But knowing "what" is not all the knowledge of content we need. We also need to think about knowing "how." Too often as teachers of the Bible we work out of a limited understanding of what knowledge is. We see it as "propositional"—in other words, as knowing *about* something or knowing *that* something is thus and so. With such a perspective, we approach our work with the Bible as propositional knowing. When we emphasize the memorization of Bible verses with children, we are often engaged in propositional knowing. We believe that if they can quote John 3:16, they therefore "know" the Bible.

Nothing is wrong with propositional knowing. We do need to know *about* things. And it is vital that as Christians we know what the Bible says. But there is more to knowing the Bible than just knowing *about* Jesus, about his life and ministry. Hopefully, knowing *how* to witness to that life and ministry in our lives today is also a goal of our teaching. We want our students to learn what it means to serve "the least of these" (Mt. 25:31–46) in our world today. Suffice it to say that knowledge of "how" is as vital as knowledge of "what" when it comes to teaching the Bible in the church.

We would be remiss in our discussion of content if we did not look briefly at two other factors that are a part of the "knowledge of content" teachers need. The first of these has to do with the "subject" we teach. Often when we talk of content, we are referring to "subject matter." By this we mean the actual material we teach, in this instance the Bible. But there are at least two other "subjects" present in the mix when we are teaching the Bible: the student and the teacher. Our students are subjects, not objects into which we are placing knowledge like making a deposit in a bank. As such, they bring their own particular life stories and perspectives into the engagement with the biblical text, and we need to respect and honor that. The knowledge of students that we discussed in the previous section becomes an important part of our knowledge of "content" when we recognize our students as subjects to whom we relate in mutual regard and respect and not objects to be manipulated and filled.

We as teachers are also subjects in the teaching context. The knowledge of self that we discussed earlier in this chapter is important to the "content" we teach. We bring our own interests and perspectives to the texts. It is simple human nature to do so. However, as Thomas Groome says, "It is when we forget what we bring to the text from our context that we read into it what we want to find there, according to our interests."[17] Understanding what we bring to the text, such as our biases and blind spots, our cultural perspectives, and so on, is important "knowledge of content" that a teacher of the Bible needs.

The remaining issue with regard to knowledge of content has to do with what Elliot Eisner calls the "three curriculums all schools teach."[18] Eisner describes it this way: "Schools teach much more—and much less—than they intend to teach. Although much of what is taught is explicit and public, a great deal is not. Indeed, it is my claim that schools provide not one curriculum to students, but three."[19] He calls these three curricula, or what we might call "content," the explicit, implicit, and null.

The explicit content refers to that which is consciously and intentionally taught. It's what we say we are teaching, such as the gospel of John. The implicit content is what we teach through the physical characteristics of the places in which we teach, the way we organize the time, the emotional environment, the way people relate to one another, whose voices are heard and whose aren't, and many other factors. Our students learn from all these whether we are aware of it or not. If we teach in ways that discourage children from asking questions of the Bible, they may learn that the Bible is not to be questioned. They then will struggle with thoughtful, in-depth study of it. Even if we never say an explicit word about not questioning, the lesson is learned anyway.

The null content refers to what we do *not* teach. This is the content that exists because it isn't there, it's left out. Our students learn from the texts we don't study as well as the ones we do. They begin to assume that what isn't studied isn't as important as the rest of the text. They learn from methods we don't use, such as the arts or role play or discussion. They assume that these aren't appropriate ways to learn scripture. Our concern with the null content isn't the absence of something. We can't teach everything. Our concern is when we haven't given thought to what we are leaving out or aren't doing. Then we are teaching in a mindless fashion, and neither our students nor the church benefit.

Knowledge of content is important for teachers of the Bible. We need to give thought to both *what* we teach and *how* we want people to know it. Attention should be paid to the different "subjects" we teach, including not only the Bible but our students and ourselves. And finally, awareness of the three contents present in any teaching situation—the explicit, implicit, and null—enables us to engage all these in ways that assist the teaching and learning we want to happen.

Knowledge of Space

We've all been in them. A classroom crowded with mismatched furniture, creaky metal folding chairs, and walls painted "institutional green." A dark youth room next to the furnace in the basement of the church. An adult Bible study space in the corner of the church fellowship hall, separated from the rest of the hall with folding screens that do not screen out the noise of people moving through the outer room. A children's church school classroom with broken toys and equipment thrown in a corner. Each of us could add our own description to the list.

Some of us have probably taught and studied the Bible in such spaces. Although we may have learned some important lessons there, we also know that too often it happened in spite of the space. Space matters! Giving thought to the space within which we teach is vital for those of us who teach the Bible.

What knowledge of space does a teacher need? Certainly an awareness of the physical space and its condition is important. Peeling paint, broken chairs and tables, old curriculum resources piled in bookcases, general dirt and grime—all these communicate a lack of awareness of the impact space has on the learning process. They say to the student, We have not given thought to your welfare; we have not prepared for your coming; and learning isn't worthy of our very best efforts.

In our discussion of the brain and how it learns, we talked about the need for enriched environments to stimulate the brain. Space rich with sights, sounds, smells, textures, and tastes helps us learn. "When you invite students into an environment that is rich with stimulants for the brain, learning happens. When you invite students into a sterile, dull, or rigid environment, learning is hampered."[20]

Our goal is to provide as pleasant a surrounding as possible for our students, space that has adequate light, comfortable temperature, and furniture and acoustics that fit their needs. We also want to give thought to how the space is arranged. Are tables and chairs grouped in ways that contribute to learning? Discussions are difficult when students are placed in rows of chairs where their initial contact with other persons is looking at the back of their heads, the least communicative part of the human body. Children crowded around a table in a small classroom with little room to move, lacking the space to role-play a Bible story, will have difficulty engaging the text in depth. Attention to physical space is important.

But there is more to space than just its physical nature. As teachers, when we think about space we also need to pay attention to qualities of space that go beyond the physical. In his work *The Courage to Teach,* Parker Palmer talks about the "paradoxes" of space, appropriate tensions that good teachers want to build into the teaching and learning space. He names six: (1) Space should be bounded and open; (2) it should be hospitable and "charged"; (3) it needs to invite the voice of the individual and the voice of the group; (4) it should honor the "little" stories of the students and the "big" stories of the disciplines and tradition; (5) it needs to support solitude and surround it with the resources of community; and (6) it needs to welcome both silence and speech.[21] Although we commend Palmer's fuller discussion of these paradoxes to you, we would like to focus attention on four of these. Teaching the Bible calls for teaching and learning space that is both open and bounded, is hospitable and charged, honors both the little and big stories, and welcomes silence and speech.

The quality of openness calls our attention to the need for learning space that is marked by an attitude of freedom and mutuality. In such space people feel free to share what they are thinking and feeling, to ask questions, to wrestle with hard issues without fear of ridicule or attack by others. Open learning space recognizes the reality that none of us has a corner on the truth, that there are different perspectives present in a given biblical text, different meanings to be drawn from the text, and different ways of reading scripture. A teacher who models openness is able to admit the limits to her own knowledge and expresses a willingness to learn along with her students.

But space without boundaries is not space but a "chaotic void,"[22] and it is difficult to learn in the midst of chaos. Therefore, our students need to know boundaries in the learning space. Boundaries provide a sense of safety, telling us what is allowed and what isn't. An obvious boundary is that violence will not be tolerated. The need to eliminate physical violence seems self-evident, but there are other ways in which we do violence to others. When we belittle or make fun of a person, refuse to hear another's viewpoint, respond to others with sarcasm and putdowns, or laugh at a child's "cute" question when he isn't trying to be funny, we are perpetuating violence. As teachers of the Bible, we must not accept such behavior.

There also need to be boundaries with regard to the content, the Bible. Not every thought or meaning a student will seek to draw from a text is appropriate. As teachers, we have a responsibility to help students stay focused, to know when an interpretation they offer moves beyond what is truly germane for a given scripture. That is why doing our homework, knowing well the text with which we work, is important. It helps us to set suitable boundaries and maintain an appropriate focus.

Learning space needs to be both hospitable and charged. "Hospitality" refers to the act of receiving others with an attitude of warmth and care; it means to make people feel welcome. People learn best when they feel safe, and hospitality offers a sense of safety and well-being. Of particular importance when teaching the Bible, hospitality means to welcome our students' different perspectives and views, to welcome new thoughts and ideas, and to receive these, not as threats, but as opportunities for all of us to learn and grow. The biblical tradition is rich with images of hospitality, of welcoming the stranger. Faithfulness to this tradition calls for nothing less in our learning spaces.

Yet hospitality alone is not enough. Although students need to feel welcomed and "at home," as Palmer says, "they must not feel so safe that they fall asleep: they need to feel the risks inherent in pursuing the deep things of the world or of the soul."[23] Challenge is critical to the brain's ability to learn, so we need to "charge" our learning spaces with stimulating questions, tasks, and experiences.

Both the "little" story of the individual student and the "big" story of the Bible and its traditions need to find a place in our learning spaces. Each of our individual students has a "story," meaning her own particular life experiences and perspectives. Our students bring these to the study of the Bible, and their stories shape how they view and interpret the text. As teachers, we need to provide opportunity for individuals to share their stories and to name their perspective on a text. They need to be able to express what they hear in a passage, to note what it means to them.

But as Palmer says, "when my little story, or yours, is our only point of reference, we easily become lost in narcissism."[24] Our individual story cannot be the only judge of what we hear in the text. We must also tell with equal care and concern the "big" story of the Bible and the scholarship and traditions that inform it. Only then can we move beyond the limits of our "little" story to see and hear in new ways that expand the meaning of the biblical text for our lives.

Finally, learning space needs to welcome both speech and silence. It goes without saying that words are important to learning. The gift of speech allows us to express thoughts and share ideas and perspectives. But sometimes we are not as aware of the importance of silence for learning. As noted in the previous chapter on the brain and learning, our brains need time to process and reflect. To fill all our learning space with words does not allow us opportunity to think about what we have seen and heard, to do the inner work we must do, to dig deeper to make a meaningful connection. Silence is not only golden, it is necessary to the learning process!

To summarize, space is important in the teaching and learning endeavor, and knowledge of space is vital for a teacher of the Bible. It is obvious we need to attend to the physical space within which we teach. But we also need to attend to other qualities of such space: how open and bounded the learning space is, the ways in which it is hospitable and charged, and the presence of both the "little" story of the individual and the "big" story of the Bible. And knowing teachers will welcome and use both speech and silence in the spaces in which they teach.

Knowledge of Teaching Models

"I have this Bible study on the gospel of Luke I have to teach in my church. I've never done this before, and I need some help as to what to do." It is a common request we both hear from our students. They have been asked to teach for the first time, and they are at a loss as to how to begin. Initially they seem to want us to share with them methods or techniques that they can use. But our approach is to invite them to step back a moment and think first about the bigger picture. What image or model of teacher do they have that informs what they think they are doing? What does the process of teaching look like? What model or approach to teaching will shape what they do? The answers to these questions need to come before they decide what teaching techniques they will use.

When we use the term *model,* or *image,* or *approach,* we are talking about the pattern that shapes what we do. An important knowledge that teachers of the Bible need is a model or approach that can guide their work and help them to know what to do when. We want to discuss two categories of models. The first is the model or image of teacher out of which we work, and the second is the model of teaching that informs our practice. Our goal here is not to claim there is one right model of teacher and teaching appropriate for everyone. Instead, we want to share some images of teacher and a model of teaching that we have found particularly helpful. Our hope is that such a discussion will encourage our readers to think about what models of teacher and teaching may be helpful and appropriate for their own practice.

Teacher

The image we carry of what a teacher is has a powerful influence on how we teach. Such images shape what we do. If we think a teacher is the "keeper of the answers,"[25] we will approach teaching as though our purpose as a teacher is to provide the answer and to have the right answer to give. But what if our answer doesn't work for others? What if they aren't asking the questions for which we have the answers? Perhaps a more helpful image of teacher is the "asker of questions," one who helps students formulate the questions they need to ask in order to discover the answers for which they search. Our own belief is that the latter image of a teacher, as an asker of questions, is a more helpful model, and it has served to inform our own work as teachers of the Bible.

What are some other images of teacher we might name that help us to think about the work of teaching in ways that truly help us to make accessible that which assists our students in learning and making meaning? Although certainly not exhaustive of such images, we can name three additional images we believe are significant to our work as teachers of the Bible: (1) guide, (2) partner, and (3) accomplice.

A teacher of the Bible is a guide. An old Teutonic word for "teacher" also means "index finger." Like an index finger, a teacher is one who points the way, who guides students through the complexities of the subject they are studying and helps them to see what they might overlook or not notice. A teacher who draws on the image of guide for his work seeks to point out significant signposts, provide commentary on what is happening and why, and help find answers to questions as they arise. Like a good tour guide, he helps to interpret and illuminate what students are seeing, hearing, feeling, and experiencing. And, like a good guide, such teachers have checked out the "trail" ahead of time, have done their own study of the text and know something of what students may see and experience.

Another helpful image of teacher is "partner." A partner is a person who has a share or part with another. Partners work alongside one another, offering and receiving insight and help from the other. Partnerships are marked by mutuality, acceptance, and equal regard. When "partner" becomes an image of teacher that shapes our practice, we see ourselves as learning along with our students. We can acknowledge that we don't have all the answers, become open to what students have to teach us, and recognize that we are learners together in this endeavor. We are able to see our students as full participants in the learning process and not objects to be manipulated and shaped any way we like. Partnering with our students in the activity of learning is an exciting image for the work of a teacher!

The final image of teacher we want to offer is that of "accomplice." It is an interesting image, not one we often associate with teachers. In our culture the word is generally used to refer to one who is a partner in crime. But when we study the derivation of the word, it comes from a Middle English term that means to succeed in doing or to bring something to pass. An accomplice is one who assists another in doing something. This seems an appropriate image for a teacher! Our work is to help our students learn, to help them accomplish learning what they need to know. As an accomplice, we don't force-feed our students facts and information, but instead help them to find out for themselves. We provide questions that invite them to think for themselves. We introduce them to Bible commentaries and concordances and show them how to use them. Rather than trying to do their learning for them (which is impossible anyway), we assist them in their efforts. A teacher of the Bible is an accomplice in the student's work of coming to know and make meaning of the biblical text.

Asker of questions, guide, partner, and accomplice—these are some of the images of teacher that invite us to think of what it is we are called to be and do in this important ministry. There are others we could mention, such as mentor, gardener, midwife, and coach. The point we want to make is the importance of becoming aware of the images of teacher that inform our work and understanding how these shape our efforts. Because these images both consciously and unconsciously influence our practice, such awareness plays a vital role in how we go about our tasks.

Teaching

Although teachers may have their favorite methods and techniques, such as storytelling or role-playing or lecturing, good teachers also have a model of teaching or an approach to teaching that helps to shape what they do and how. Such a model is an informed, reflective way of teaching that offers an overall guide to the teaching process and provides us with something like a road map for what we are doing. One of the models of teaching that we have found particularly helpful is an approach developed by Thomas Groome called "shared Christian praxis."[26] We believe this model takes seriously much of what we have been saying about how people learn, about who our students are, and about how we are to work with our content and relate as teachers.

Shared Christian praxis is a "participative and dialogical"[27] approach to teaching that engages both students and teacher in the process of "accessing" the biblical story, drawing meaning and insight from the story, and responding to this with lives of lived faith in the world. The terms *participative* and *dialogical* are key to this approach. It calls for the full participation of both students and teachers in the learning moment. Students are not passive receptacles, simply waiting to be filled by the teacher. They are full participants in the process. And other voices, not just the teacher's, are engaged and heard. Teacher, student, and the Bible all become a part of the give-and-take dialogue that occurs.

This model of teaching is made up of five steps, or movements. The term *movement* is used to reflect the dynamic and fluid nature of this approach. It is not a rigid set of steps through which a teacher moves students, but is more like a dance in which the movements overlap, repeat, and combine in different ways. There is as much art as there is science to the shared Christian praxis approach.

For our work as teachers of the Bible, the five movements can be described as follows:

1. *Naming/Expressing Present Practice*
   The first movement in this teaching approach invites the participants to name and express their "present praxis," or understanding of the text being explored. They are encouraged to express their own feelings, attitudes, beliefs, values, perceptions, assessments, thoughts, and so on with regard to the biblical text. As a teacher, it is important to remember that our students need an opportunity to do this in their own words and in a variety of ways. Sometimes the expression can take an artistic form, such as a picture, a song, a poem, or a movement. Sometimes it will be a simple discussion regarding what the students hear in the text being studied. What do they think, believe, feel, or care about this text? One of the key things to remember is that students should not be forced or even subtly coerced to say or express something they do not believe, think, or feel.

2. *Critical Reflection on Present Practice*
   The second movement in shared Christian praxis encourages students to go beyond the surface into deeper reflection. It invites them to move from an uncritical acceptance of what they think, believe, and feel about the text under study to a more carefully thought-through understanding of their feelings, attitudes, beliefs, and so on. They are encouraged to make sense of what they believe and to explore why they believe it. As a part of this movement, the teacher invites students to use three important skills of reflection: (1) reason, (2) memory, and (3) imagination.

The skill of reasoning calls students to a critical analysis of their present thinking in order to take note of what influences their thinking and action, what assumptions they are making and why, and what is really being expressed in the feelings, attitudes, beliefs, and values that have been named. A question such as

"Why do you think you might believe that?" can be a helpful tool, taking care that our tone of voice does not communicate a demand to justify what we believe. Even children can be asked to think about why they believe what they do.

To call on students' memory asks them to think about the roots of their current beliefs and attitudes. It is a kind of personal archaeology that is more than just recalling something to mind. To engage memory, a teacher might ask a student to recall when they first remembered hearing about or thinking what they currently think. This part of critical reflection is asking where the current beliefs and attitudes come from. Such knowledge of the past helps us to decide whether our thoughts and beliefs are still appropriate in the present.

By using imagination, people are invited to think about the consequences of their current way of understanding. What difference does it make if I think this way? What are other alternatives and possibilities? This aspect of critical reflection is not just idle wonderment, but a creative imagining of what might be, of other ways of looking at the text and its meanings. It offers students an opportunity to consider the future, to become aware of the consequences, the possibilities, and the responsibilities in their present thinking and beliefs.

3. *Making Accessible the Biblical Text*

Although the whole shared Christian praxis approach is a way of making accessible according to the definition of teaching we have been using in this chapter, the third movement specifically focuses on making accessible or opening up for our students the text under study. This movement calls for the use of careful exegetical skills, inviting students into a more thorough look at the text, the ways in which they are "reading" the text (we will talk more about reading in chapter 4), the biases and cultural perspectives that both teacher and students bring to the text, and how one discerns between a false and an authentic explanation of the text.

We need to engage this movement in ways that *disclose* the text as fully as possible. We also need to be *dialogical,* inviting other voices and perspectives into the conversation. And as teachers, we should seek to be *engaging,* drawing our students into the learning moment and not doing all the work of making accessible ourselves. Helping our students develop good exegetical skills is a vital part of teaching the Bible.

4. *Dialectical Integration of the Biblical Text with the Students' Lives and Practice*

   This movement puts the biblical text into dialogue with the students' lives and practice that were named in movements 1 and 2. The goal is an integration of the two. It is important that this be a "dialectical," or dialogical, process in which both the text and the student are heard and encountered with mutual respect. Students are asked to consider how the text affirms, questions, and calls them beyond their present practice and understanding. They are also asked how their present practice and understanding affirms, reshapes, and critically appropriates the text.

5. *Deciding and Responding*

   The final movement explicitly challenges students to make decisions, drawing on insights gained from previous movements of the process. They are encouraged to decide how they will now live in response to what they have learned. Key questions are "What now?"; "What difference does this text make in my life?"; and "How might I live in response to this text?"

Although certainly not the only model of teaching, the shared Christian praxis approach does offer us a pattern for carrying out the activities of teaching in a coherent and thoughtful manner. Whatever model one chooses, we believe that it is vital for the work of a good teacher to have a model of teaching and to be aware of the images of teacher that inform how we approach our work. Such teacher knowledge is critical to our efforts.

Knowledge of Methods and Techniques

"What do I do?" Let's return to the student's question in the previous section. It continues to be an important question and points to our final category of teacher knowledges, that of methods and techniques. Although we certainly believe that good teachers need the "bigger" picture we've just discussed, they also need a repertoire of methods and techniques from which they can draw for teaching. By methods and techniques we mean those specific activities we use in the teaching moment.

There are certainly many methods, techniques, and tools a teacher can use. In fact, there are probably as many of these as there are teachers who use them. Therefore, our purpose in this section is not to name the "best" methods, techniques, and tools, nor is it to provide our readers with an exhaustive list. Instead, we believe it is more helpful to consider some basic principles or guidelines that help us to select the methods we use. What do we need to consider when we choose our methods and tools for teaching?

1. *Our methods, techniques, and tools need to be appropriate for the content, the context, and the people we teach.* When selecting a teaching method, we need to think about the content we are teaching. What is this text all about? What would be the most helpful way in which to engage it? To illustrate, recall the story of the bent-over woman in Luke 13 and Karen's use of an embodiment method in which she asked the students to walk bent over in order to experience what it was like for this woman. To just discuss (certainly an appropriate method at times) what it means to be bent over doesn't accomplish the same encounter with the text that the actual experience of being bent over does. Selecting a method appropriate for a text is key.

When selecting a method, we need to think about the context in which we teach. What physical resources are available, and what is absent? In what kind of setting will we be working? To choose to role-play a story that calls for a lot of movement and space when the class is being taught in a small, cramped room filled with tables and chairs is to choose an inappropriate method for that context.

Knowledge of the people we are teaching is also critical when selecting a method. To use the bent-over woman illustration again, it would be very inappropriate to use the method described if one were working with a group of senior adults with mobility problems. They already have a point of identification with this woman! We also need to think carefully about children when selecting methods for teaching them. Arts and crafts projects are often a part of Bible study with young children. Too often these projects require them to use fine motor skills they have not yet fully developed. Doing dramatizations in which children are able to use their whole bodies in acting out a story is far more appropriate. We need to think about our students—who they are; what their physical abilities, cognitive abilities, and learning styles are; how their brains work—when selecting our methods, making sure methods and students are compatible.

2. *The broader the repertoire of methods, techniques, and tools we have, the better.* A variety of methods is important. A key reason has to do with the people we teach. As just mentioned, we need methods that are appropriate for our students. Because our students come with different abilities, learning styles, and so on, variety is essential to be able to engage them all in the learning process. Visual learners need to see pictures, illustrations, videos, displays, and demonstrations. Aural learners need opportunities to listen and to verbalize. Kinesthetic learners need to be physically engaged, involved in role plays and other hands-on activities. Interactive students need to work with others. The broader our repertoire of methods, the more likely it is that we will teach in ways that are appropriate for all our students.

3. *Be familiar with and give careful thought to a new method, technique, or tool before using it.* It is important as teachers that we know how to use the methods and tools we select. We have observed that our seminary students sometimes select a method they have read about in a book without actually trying that method or having experienced it themselves. Or they select a piece of music or a video without thinking carefully about how it might be heard and interpreted. They then wonder why the teaching session becomes a disaster. They simply weren't prepared to know how people might respond and what was actually involved in using that particular technique or tool.

In one of our teaching experiences, we used a video presentation of the story of the Gerasene demoniac (Mk. 5:1–20). We had both been quite moved when we saw it but had not thought carefully enough about how our students might interpret the images portrayed. We encountered some intense and angry reactions to the images presented that prevented some of the students from engaging fully in the learning experience. Although we did not stop using that particular video, we did spend time after that encounter giving careful thought to how to present it, what the responses might be, and how we would reply. Methods do take on a life of their own, and giving careful thought to where they might lead is important.

4. *Remember that the purpose of a method, technique, or tool is to assist the student in learning.* Certainly, methods are to help people learn! However, we've observed other reasons at work in selecting methods. These include (1) because "we've always done it that way," (2) in order to "look good," and (3) to duplicate an experience.

Sometimes we select a method simply because it is the one we always use, not because it helps us teach in ways that our students learn. We've simply always done it this way and don't stop to ask whether it is appropriate for this content, context, and group of students. Sometimes a method is chosen because it "looks good." We see this in our seminary students who want to be "with it" and be known as a teacher with the "newest approach" or one who is up-to-date on the "latest thing." It doesn't matter whether the method helps the people in that particular teaching setting. It's all about "looking good" as a teacher.

Sometimes we want to duplicate an experience we have had and we think that we can do this by using the same methods. Remember the seminary student we described earlier who wanted her college-age students to have the same experience in Bible study that she had had in seminary. What she discovered was that duplicating experiences simply does not work and that choosing methods on that basis is not appropriate. Instead, the most important criterion for selecting our methods, techniques, and tools is whether they help the students we teach learn.

Although guidelines for selecting teaching methods are vitally important, we would be remiss in this discussion if we did not at least mention what we consider to be one of the most basic methods that needs to be in every teacher's repertoire. This is the use of questions. Questions are a core method of teaching. They are readily available, cost nothing in terms of money or resources, and can be used with all ages. But they do require some thought and preparation. Knowing how to ask the right question is important.

At least three different kinds of questions can be used in the teaching process: information questions, analytical questions, and integrative questions.[28] Information questions are simply that—questions that ask for information. "What are the books of the

Bible?" "In Luke 2, where did Joseph and Mary go to be registered?" and "What is the 'fruit of the Spirit' in Galatians 5:22–23?" are all examples of information questions. Such questions ask for basic information and are important in a teacher's repertoire because they help us get a sense of what our students are retaining.

But information questions alone are not enough to help students grow and learn. Analytical questions push students deeper into the text and invite them to think more critically about what they are reading. Such questions do not assume right answers and are more open, with the potential for different responses. They invite the student to go beyond mere recall of facts and information to an analysis of what those facts and information might mean. Examples of analytical questions are "In what ways do you think the church today is like the church Paul was addressing in his letter to the Galatians?"; "Why might Moses have been reluctant to return to Egypt to free the Hebrew people?"; and "What do you think Mary was feeling as she journeyed to Nazareth with Joseph?"

Finally, information and analytical questions alone do not fully assist our students in making their own connections with the text and drawing from it meaning for their own lives. Integrative questions are an important tool for this. Integrative questions are related to students' own life experiences and ask them to make a value judgment about something, to say what it means to them. As with analytical questions, there are no right answers, and the questions are broad and open ended. They are the kind of questions that encourage students to go beyond information and analysis to engage the text in transformational ways. Examples of such questions are "If you had been one of the shepherds on the hillside in Luke 2, what would you have done?"; "In what ways do you see the fruit of the Spirit present in your own life?"; and "Like Moses, are you being called to an act of liberation? What might God be calling you to do?"

Knowledge of methods and techniques is vital for a teacher of the Bible. Although the methods and techniques from which we can draw are many and varied, it is important to have some guidelines to make our selection. Making sure they are appropriate for our students, our content, and our setting is crucial. Having personal experience with them and knowing how to use them are both important. Remembering that the purpose of any method, technique, or tool is to help students learn is vital. And finally, knowing how to use and ask the right question is at the core of good teaching. All this is significant knowledge for those who are called to teach the Bible in the church.

Summary and Implications for Teaching the Bible

How we teach is not about acquiring the latest method or using the newest technique. Good teachers learn to teach by knowing themselves, their students, their content, how to create good teaching space, the images of teacher and models of teaching from which they can draw, and how to select methods appropriate for the task. Given these core teacher knowledges, what important implications might we name for teaching the Bible in the church? In closing, we want to name six and invite our readers to ponder these for their own ministries of teaching.

1. *Know thyself. How* we teach depends on *who* we are. It is important to know what motivates us, what our own particular biases and favored ways of reading scripture are, what our learning style is, and what unique gifts and graces we bring to the task of teaching. Whether consciously or unconsciously, all of these shape how we teach, and intentional attention to them can only strengthen our endeavors.

2. How *we teach depends on* who *we are teaching*. Students of the Bible come in all sizes and shapes. How we teach them depends on how they learn, where they are in their biological and cognitive development, what kinds of personalities they have, and how they have been shaped by their particular cultures. Remember that we teach *people,* and knowing who they are is central to how we teach.

3. How *we teach depends on* where *we teach*. Much of teaching is the creating of space in which learning can take place. It is obvious that attending to the physical space—making sure it is clean, pleasant, safe, welcoming, appropriate for the students' needs, and filled with enriching materials and activities—is important. But we also need to take note of other qualities of space, including its openness and its boundaries, how it welcomes and how it challenges, ways in which both the "little" and the "big" story are included, and how speech and silence are both present.

4. *Know your content.* To teach the Bible, one must be a student of the Bible and engage in critical study of it. Nothing replaces doing our homework when preparing to teach a text. In addition to knowing this subject matter, it is also important to know the other subjects present in the teaching setting. Knowledge of self and of students is a key part of knowing content. And finally, awareness of the implicit and null content we teach by who we are, where we are, and what we don't talk about or do plays a vital role in how we teach.

5. *How we teach is shaped by the images of teacher we hold and by the approach to teaching we use.* Each of us carries an image or images of what we think a teacher is. It may be an answer giver, guide, partner, accomplice, or something else. Our image may be of an actual teacher, and we try to pattern our work after him or her. Whatever images we hold and wherever they come from, it is important that we be aware of them and reflect on whether they are helpful or not. The same is true of our approach to teaching. We operate, often unconsciously, out of a model of teaching. Being aware of our model and seeking to educate ourselves about other models is important work for a teacher of the Bible.

6. *Knowing how to choose and when to use a method, tool, or technique is key.* Choosing and using methods depend on their appropriateness for our students, content, and setting. Choosing and using methods depend on our knowledge of and experience with them. Choosing and using the right question are foundational to good teaching. And at the heart of it all is remembering that the purpose of any method, tool, or technique is to help students learn.

3

Teaching the Bible: An Intercultural Education Experience

I sit here listening to the men around me chew their ears of corn. They eat corn like a snack and it is much tougher than our ears of corn. We are staying in Mbete at the guest house—a new grass hut with a dirt floor...Today has been like no experience in my life! Seventy kilometers on a dirt road, sometimes only two tracks through the grass. We are truly in rural Africa here...I find some difficulty in trying to write—things happen so quickly, we have seen so much, I can't sort it all out. Driving across the savannah yesterday. Space like I have never seen! The horizon is clear for 360 degrees! People crowding around where ever we stop. All of them looking and staring. And how very poor the village is. Water is carried from a stream three-quarters of a mile away...Such a different way of life. I don't think I could really adequately describe it to any one who hasn't been here.

These words from a journal Karen kept during a 1991 trip to Zaire (now the Democratic Republic of Congo) describe a profound and life-changing intercultural education experience in her life. It is our claim that teaching the Bible in the church is also an intercultural education experience with the same complex dynamics and the same life-changing potential. Understanding this claim has significant implications for our work as teachers in the church.

What do we mean by "intercultural education experience"? We mean an educational experience involving several cultures. Teaching the Bible calls for the encounter of several cultures, including the culture of the student, the culture of the teacher, the church culture, the wider social culture, the cultures of the texts themselves, and finally the culture envisioned by the texts. All of these are at play in any teaching encounter, and we think they have an important impact on the teaching task before us.

In this chapter we want to explore the intercultural nature of teaching the Bible. We begin with a look at intercultural education, what it is and how we do it. Then we explore the various layers of culture at work in our encounters with scripture, focusing specifically on Western culture, ecclesial or church culture, and the cultures of the Bible. Our purpose here is to raise awareness about the cultural lenses we bring to the Bible and the cultural lenses we encounter there. Further, we want to offer assistance for teachers regarding how to engage these cultural issues with our students.

Intercultural Education

Before exploring the nature of intercultural education, we believe it is important first to consider a question we always pose for our students: Why is it important to talk about intercultural education when exploring teaching the Bible in the church? Our initial answer is quite simple. The stories and witness of the Bible come from other times and places, from cultures other than our own, and just opening its pages is to step into an intercultural experience. As Lesslie Newbigin, in talking about the gospel and therefore the Bible, says:

> [The gospel] is itself culturally conditioned…Neither at the beginning, nor at any subsequent time, is there or can there be a gospel that is not embodied in a culturally conditioned form of words. The idea that one can or could at any time separate out by some process of distillation a pure gospel unadulterated by any cultural accretions is an illusion…Every statement of the gospel in words is conditioned by the culture of which those words are a part…There can never be a culture-free gospel.[1]

To study and teach the Bible is an intercultural education experience, though we often do not recognize this.

In addition to the basic reality that teaching the Bible *is* an engagement in intercultural education, there is another reason for our framing this task as such. This has to do with our belief that teaching the Bible calls for both *retrieval* and *appropriation* of the biblical witness. By retrieval, we are talking about the work of uncovering and recovering insights from an ancient culture. The Bible emerged from worlds different from our own, and "spoken in different worlds, specific words mean different things."[2] To understand what these texts might be saying to us is not an automatic or easy task. But retrieval alone is not enough. We also want our students to appropriate, to make their own, these insights that come from a distant people and place and from an ancient text.

To engage in retrieval and appropriation as we teach the Bible, we believe that some knowledge of intercultural education is important. Such knowledge helps us to think about how we enter another culture and become aware of it, about some of the stages through which a student moves as they engage another culture, and about the ways in which we learn from other cultures and discover the insights they have to offer. In order to retrieve and appropriate, we must develop awareness of another culture and know how to learn from it. All of this has important implications for the ways in which we teach.

To begin our look at intercultural education, some definitions are in order. The first is a definition of "culture." What is it we are engaging in inter*cultural* education? The following definition has proven helpful for our work:

> Culture is the sum total of ways of living, including values, beliefs, esthetic standards, linguistic expression, patterns of thinking, behavioral norms, and styles of communication which a group of people has developed to assure its survival in a particular physical and human environment.[3]

"Culture" refers to our social heredity as opposed to our biological one. In other words, culture is learned. But we begin learning it from the moment we are born, and it functions almost as though it is biological. Our cultural perspective seems as natural as our breathing.

Milton Bennett says culture is more a process than a thing. One does not have a culture so much as one lives or engages in a culture.[4] We believe this is an important perspective on culture. Culture is not so much a thing we possess as it is a life we live. We don't put on our culture or discard it like an article of clothing. We live it and we express it in our every movement. And we do this with seldom a thought about it.

To think of teaching the Bible as an *inter*cultural experience reminds us that the biblical texts come from different times and places than our own and that the study of scripture involves an encounter with these different cultures. We are drawn particularly to the term "*inter*cultural" because it calls to our attention the reality that reading and studying the Bible involves the interaction, the meeting together, of various cultures. It helps us remember that the people who authored these texts had their own identity, language, systems of nonverbal communication, material culture, history, and ways of thinking, of making meaning, and of doing things. These are unique to those cultures and more often than not are different from ours. To forget this often leads to misunderstandings of biblical texts. We hear them as belonging to *our* culture rather than the *ancient* cultures where they originated.

One of the major difficulties comes when we forget cultural uniqueness and try to say that people are really all alike. Then we miss some of the important cultural factors that shaped any particular biblical text and risk misreading that text in the cultural setting of our own day and time. We will say more about these differences later in this chapter, but it is important now to note that overlooking such difference makes it more difficult to understand and learn from another culture. As Edward Hall, a noted anthropologist says, "The 'they are just like the folks back home' syndrome is one of the most persistent and widely held misconceptions of the Western world, if not the whole world."[5] This misconception leads to much misunderstanding and, in terms of studying the Bible, misreading of texts.

Intercultural education is rooted in the knowledge that there *are* differences among cultures. By definition, such education is *the process of preparing persons to live and work effectively in cultures other than their own.*[6] Although certainly we cannot actually live and work in those ancient cultures, we do have to engage them when teaching the Bible, and intercultural education helps us prepare our students to do this. What, then, are the major steps, or movements, in this process? We name three major movements in the work of intercultural education: (1) developing awareness of our own cultural framework, (2) developing awareness of the other culture, and (3) developing intercultural competence.[7]

1. *Developing awareness of our own cultural framework.* "The first step toward understanding another culture is becoming aware of one's own cultural habits and values."[8] We are all culturally embedded creatures. One of the hardest things to do, however, is to name our own culture. As an ancient Chinese proverb says, "If you want a definition of water, don't ask a fish." As students of the Bible, our own cultural dependence is so strong that we often don't realize the cultural lenses through which we are reading biblical texts. We all have "selective perception," which means we see what we have been taught to see. This is at work in any intercultural encounter, including teaching the Bible, and it often means that we miss some important insights.

One of the significant tasks in intercultural education is to develop awareness of oneself as a cultural being. One of the ways we do this with our students is to have them create a collage of the cultural "ocean" in which they swim. Using clippings and pictures from magazines and newspapers, they prepare a visual representation of their own cultural context. This helps them begin to *see* more clearly the cultural values that shape them. What complicates this, however, is the presence of both "overt" and "covert" cultural dynamics in each of us. Some of our cultural dynamics are evident and clear. In their collages it is easy for the students to name the materialism, consumerism, competition, and emphasis on the individual that are obvious values in our North American context. What is more difficult to name is the "covert" culture, "those myriad of implicit rules that regulate our everyday lives."[9] These are those taken-for-granted ways of seeing and being in the world. For example, whereas our students can often name "individualism" as a cultural value, they easily miss some of the implications of this. We illustrate this by asking them what they first think of when they hear the pronoun *you.* Their usual response is that they think of *me,* the singular form of *you*. When we go on to point out that in biblical texts "you" often means "you all," they begin to see how their cultural perspective leads them to risk missing the deeply communal nature of these texts, texts concerned more with the community than individuals.

To teach the Bible in the church, we need to be aware of our cultural biases and the ways in which these shape what we see, hear, and understand in the biblical text. For American Protestants, this includes an awareness of Western culture, of the cultural ocean that is the United States, and of the ecclesial, or church, culture within which we live. All these "layers" of culture, about which we will say more later, work together to form the cultural framework out of which we approach the study of scripture. Recognizing that teaching the Bible is an intercultural education experience challenges us to develop awareness of this cultural ocean within which we swim and through which we read the text.

2. *Developing awareness of the other culture*. The second movement in intercultural education is the development of an awareness of the other culture or cultures we are engaging. Too often "[w]e assume that people of another culture or subculture see, feel, and think as we do. It is true that certain basic emotions, such as joy and sorrow, are common to all cultures but the ways of expressing these feelings may not be the same. Much misunderstanding is caused by the assumption that our own reactions are universal."[10]

To learn from another culture, we have to have an understanding of it. Our own experience tells us that too often when teaching the Bible, we overlook this need to become aware of the cultural perspectives out of which the text comes. We too easily assume this is "our" book and that the people who shaped the Bible are "just like us." They aren't! And to learn from them, we need to have some understanding of them.

An important aspect of developing awareness of another culture involves what Milton Bennett calls "intercultural sensitivity."[11] In intercultural education we seek to become sensitive to cultural differences and to validate those differences. This is not always easy for those of us deeply embedded in Western culture, who often see non-Western perspectives as less developed—more primitive—than our own, and thus to be disdained. In developing awareness of another culture, we must do so with affirmation, appreciation, and respect.

The significant question for those of us who teach the Bible in the church is, How can we help our students become familiar with cultures that no longer exist in "real time"? One of the obvious ways one becomes familiar with another culture today is to go and live in that culture, spending time with the people. Such opportunities do not exist when studying the Bible. Those ancient cultures are no longer available for us to spend time in.

Realizing the difficulty of coming to know another culture even when we can live there for an extended time, we still believe there are some helpful ways to begin to open up the ancient cultures of the Bible for our students. The use of imagination is critical. One of the gifts humans have is the ability to be some place in their minds that they can't be physically. We can help our students imagine another time and think about what it would have been like in ancient Israel or ancient Palestine or the ancient Greco-Roman world. Through the use of imagination we can regularly place a biblical text in its cultural context, inviting students to "imagine what it was like when..." even as we remind them to be aware that their own cultural biases may be shaping the picture.

Because of the danger that our own cultural biases will cloud our imaginations, we have found it very helpful to assist our imagining through the use of carefully designed simulations and participatory experiences, what Gary Weaver calls "contrast-culture" exercises.[12] We witnessed such a participatory experience being used by two of our students in a class assignment one day. They had been asked to introduce the class to the cultures of the ancient Near East. Being aware of the deeply patriarchal nature of these cultures, the students decided to engage the class in an experience of patriarchy by preparing and serving a meal as it might have been done in that time. The students, both women, served the food, but they only served it to the men in the class. It was as though the women class members did not exist. The women in the class found their shock at being ignored was compounded because of their experience in this culture, where women are often served first. Through participation in this exercise, all the students gained a deeper sense of the shape of patriarchy in those ancient times and a better understanding of the cultural values and customs out of which the texts they were reading came.

Developing awareness of other cultures is an important part of intercultural education. It calls us to be aware that there are differences and to be sensitive to and respect those differences. As teachers, it invites us to use imagination as a vital tool for helping students develop awareness of other people, places, and times, and it challenges us to design simulations and participatory exercises that enable us to catch a glimpse of what life in another culture might have been like.

3. *Developing intercultural competence.* The final movement in intercultural education is the development of intercultural competence. Intercultural competence refers to the ability to move among cultures. Such competence is important for students of the Bible because we are called to move between our own culture and time and the cultures and times of the Bible as we seek to learn from this ancient story. It is hoped that as teachers of the Bible, we want our students to be able to engage the various cultures involved in the study of scripture and to do so in ways that lead to their own growth and transformation.

This intercultural competence develops by way of a series of stages through which students seem to move as they begin to acquire an awareness of the cultural complexity involved in studying the Bible.[13] These stages are (1) denial, (2) defense, (3) minimization, (4) acceptance, (5) adaptation, and (6) integration. Not all students move through every one of these stages in a linear process, but we have seen this process happen often enough in seminary and church that we believe an awareness of it is helpful to teachers of the Bible.

Denial is the refusal to grant the truth of something. We have observed students of the Bible in both the seminary and the church begin their journey in intercultural education by denying that there really are any differences between cultures. In effect, this is what many people who read the Bible literally are doing. They are saying that the words on the page say exactly what we think they say and that there are no differences that we must consider as we read the text.

But not all those in a denial stage are literalists. Karen observed this one morning in an adult Sunday school class. The class was studying Peter's confession about Jesus found in Matthew 16:13–20, where Peter declares that Jesus is the Messiah. The class was asked what the term *messiah* meant to them. One woman commented that Peter, as a first-century Jew, probably understood this term differently than we would. Another class member, a man who generally was not a literal reader of the text, strongly disagreed with her. He was convinced that there really wasn't any difference in what Peter meant and what we might mean and he spent some time arguing his point. At that moment he was caught in denial of the cultural differences that needed to be considered.

Educational strategies for people in this stage include the kind of "contrast-culture" experiences we discussed when talking about developing awareness of the other culture. As teachers, our goal is the simple recognition that differences do exist, that people of another time and place may not have seen the world exactly as we do. Helping people move beyond denial of cultural differences is an important task in teaching the Bible.

Moving people out of denial does not end our work. From denial we have watched people move to *defense,* the next point in developing intercultural competence. Defense differs from denial in that people do recognize cultural differences, but they create defenses against having to take them seriously and engage them. This "defending" can take several forms. Sometimes it is revealed in a denigrating or belittling of the other culture. We hear this in comments such as, "The world of the Old Testament is just all about war and violence, and I'm so glad that as Christians we focus on the New Testament, which moves beyond that."

Actually this comment reveals two forms of defense. The first part of the statement negatively stereotypes or denigrates the cultures out of which the Old Testament emerged, and the second part casts the world of the New Testament in a superior light. Superiority, or the claim that something is of a higher value, is another way we defend. By feeling superior, we don't have to take seriously the culture of another and what we might learn from it.

Learning to affirm and respect another culture in its own right helps to lower our defenses, but it also does not end the work of developing intercultural competence. We have observed students of the Bible move from defending their own culture to another stage in this developmental process, a stage called *minimization*. In this stage cultural differences are trivialized. Students no longer deny there are differences, nor do they feel they have to defend their own cultural perspective. Instead, what they do is adopt an attitude that those differences really don't mean anything.

Comments such as, "Deep down inside we are really all alike" and "In the final analysis, we are all children of God" can be a signal of minimization. The problem with the first comment is that those basic things we highlight as being the same almost always come out of our own culture, the assumption being that everyone is really just like *me*. And although there is truth in the claim that we are all God's children, that doesn't mean that we have the same understanding of who "God" is and what a "child" is and therefore share a common meaning when we make this claim.

Often, people who seek to trivialize cultural differences adopt an attitude of "physical universalism." Basically, they claim that humans are biological creatures, and that makes us all alike. The problem with this stance is that our identity as humans is shaped not only by our biology but also by the cultural contexts within which we live as biological creatures. What we understand to be "basically human" is still filtered through a cultural lens. "For many people in minimization, lack of awareness of their own culture underlies the assumption of cultural similarity. When they can place more of their own behavior in a cultural context, they are less inclined to assume that the behavior is universal."[14]

Denial, defense, and minimization are all ways in which we discount cultural differences. We hope that through careful study, the use of imagination, engagement in simulations and experiences, and the use of other tools of cultural encounter, we can help our students become aware of and open to the cultural differences that are present as we seek to understand and draw meaning from these ancients texts.

As people move beyond these stages of denial, defense, and minimization, we begin to see the next stage in developing intercultural competence, that of *acceptance* of cultural difference. Acceptance is marked by a respect for cultural differences. It is seen in a recognition that our own worldview is a cultural construction and a willingness to admit that our ancient ancestors might have seen and done things differently. It leads to a reluctance to step quickly into the pages of the Bible and say this is "our" story. Instead, students realize that historical critical study of the text and its culture is important and necessary in order for meaning relevant to our day and time to emerge.

But mere acceptance is not enough if we want our students to have intercultural competency. Beyond acceptance, we also want our students to search out knowledge about the cultural context of the Bible and to ask thoughtful questions as to how this context might have shaped a particular text. We want them to move beyond acceptance to the next stage of intercultural competence, that of *adaptation*.

Adaptation is the process of adjusting to or changing in relationship to a given situation. In terms of intercultural education, adaptation means that one not only recognizes and accepts cultural differences but also works to develop a deeper comprehension and understanding of those differences. It means we develop skills for relating to and engaging a worldview different from our own.

An important step in adaptation is empathy, the ability to have some sense of feeling for another's perspective. Although we can never truly understand another culture from the perspective of one native to that culture, we can spend time and effort in imagining what it might be like to walk in the other's shoes. Although the inability to actually spend time in the ancient cultures of the Bible is a stumbling block for cultural empathy, we can still engage in experiences that open us to what it might have been like in those times. The exercise described earlier in which our students sought to help us understand the patriarchy of the ancient Eastern world is a good example.

Adaptation enables us to look at a text from more than one cultural frame of reference. Our repertoire of cultural alternatives is increased, and we find it easier to view a text from a perspective other than just the one we bring to it. It means we begin to hear that pronoun *you*, as in "You have heard it said," and know that it can mean both "me" and "us."

The final point in the development of intercultural competence is *integration*. Integration involves our ability to be both a *part of* and *apart from* a given cultural context. Persons who have grown to the point of integration in intercultural competence are aware of and are able to name their own cultural perspective (they are the fish who can define water), are able to critique that cultural perspective and see how it limits them, and at least to some small degree, are able to stand in another cultural place and see and understand the world from that perspective.

For teachers of the Bible, integration calls us regularly to invite our students to self-reflection. We help them name the ocean of culture within which they swim. We challenge them no longer to assume a cultural common ground as they explore a text. We help them explore the cultural differences that exist, inviting them to treat these differences with respect and to guard against a mindless collapsing of these differences. We call them to move toward integration, knowing that transformative understanding and meaning only come when the challenging work of intercultural education is taking place.

We need to say one final, brief word about intercultural education before moving on to a discussion of the various layers of culture involved in teaching the Bible. "Most cultural exploration begins with the annoyance of being lost."[15] We have sometimes seen this sense of being lost present in our students when we first introduce the intercultural nature of teaching the Bible. One of the ways this annoyance seems to manifest itself is through feelings of "culture shock." What is culture shock, and how we might address it in helpful ways?

Culture shock is defined as "any physical or emotional discomfort experienced by those adjusting to a new environment."[16] It often involves feelings of disorientation and discomfort. Sometimes these feelings lead to resistance on the part of students to exploring cultural dynamics, and they argue instead that we should "just read the Bible and not worry about all this other stuff." They become entrenched in their traditional ways of reading scripture and resist changing.

What might teachers do when they witness culture shock in those they teach? A good place to begin is helping students become aware that what they are experiencing *is* a form of culture shock. In reality, we are asking students to see things from a different perspective and adapt to other cultural viewpoints. Naming this and suggesting that culture shock may be a natural response to this experience can help to alleviate some of the anxiety and discomfort. Sharing our own experiences of facing something new and unfamiliar and what helped us cope is another step we can take as teachers. Providing a sense of safe space in which students can face their disorientation and discomfort is also key. People make adjustments more easily when they are feeling "pulled" into a new perspective rather than being "pushed." Inviting people to consider another cultural viewpoint rather than demanding it is one way of pulling rather than pushing. Remembering that all of this takes time is vitally important. We do not develop intercultural competence overnight. It is a process that requires patience and understanding on the part of the teacher.

Contemporary Cultures

As we have indicated, an awareness of one's own cultural framework is essential to intercultural competence. If we and those whom we teach are going to engage the Bible seriously, we will need to be aware of the cultures in which we participate, as well as the cultures of the biblical world. Because intercultural education begins with an awareness of one's own cultural framework, we believe it is appropriate to begin this discussion of the cultural layers we encounter when teaching and studying the Bible with a sketch of some of the contemporary cultural frameworks in which we participate.

We believe there are three dimensions of our contemporary cultural framework of which a student of the Bible needs to be aware. Most broadly, those of us in the United States are part of Western culture, a way of living that developed in Western Europe in the 1700s under the influence of an intellectual movement called the Enlightenment. Although some of the values, norms, and ways of thinking that have characterized Western culture for almost 300 years are now being challenged, our culture remains heavily influenced by the Enlightenment. Second, we also need to be aware of the culture of the United States. Although significantly influenced by Western culture, uniquely American experiences have shaped the culture of the United States. It is possible to distinguish an American culture— a way of living and thinking particular to the United States—as a

distinctive subset of Western culture. Finally, we also need to consider the church cultures in which we participate. These ecclesial
cultures, impacted by Western culture and the culture of the United
States, also have unique contours that affect teaching the Bible.

Of course, to describe Western, American (United States), or
Protestant church cultures in any depth would require a very long
discussion that is much beyond the scope of this book. Instead, we
offer a brief overview of some of the cultural issues that confront
anyone who teaches the Bible in a congregation in the United
States. Our discussion is intended to be illustrative and not
comprehensive, and to raise issues about the ways that teaching the
Bible is an intercultural experience. Those who want to teach the
Bible well will need to become students of many cultures—the
multiple contemporary cultures in which we participate, as well as
the multiple cultures that are reflected in the Bible.

Western Culture (Modernity)

Much of Western Europe and North America share a common
cultural heritage that started to take distinctive shape in Europe
almost 300 years ago. This culture—ways of living, thinking, and
valuing—is still powerfully influential in our time. What decisively
shaped that which we now know as Western culture (or, as it is often
called, modernity) is the Enlightenment. Although Western culture,
or modernity, is a complex phenomenon, the core of this cultural
expression is summarized by Marcus Borg in the following points:

1. First, modernity is characterized by scientific ways of
    knowing...We know something to be true today through
    experimentation and verification.

2. Second, modernity is marked by what is sometimes called "the
    modern worldview" or "the Newtonian worldview"...The
    modern worldview is based on scientific ways of knowing:
    What is real is that which can be known through the methods
    of science.

3. The modern worldview yields a material understanding of
    reality. What is real is the space-time world of matter and
    energy. Reality is made up of tiny bits and pieces of "stuff," all

of them interacting with one another in accord with "natural laws." The result is a picture of the universe as a closed system of cause and effect.[17]

Borg's three points capture much of what is central to the way we and most people in churches today view the world.

Lesslie Newbigin, although largely in agreement with Borg, stresses the crucial role of reason in Western culture. At the heart of the Enlightenment culture of which we are a part is the assumption that by reason (the analytic capacity of mathematics and science) humans can come to an understanding and mastery of the world.[18] What is "true" needs to be objectively verified and proven by supporting "data," facts that can be duplicated in controlled experiments.

There is much to be appreciated about the Enlightenment and our modern worldview. Advances in medicine and science are directly attributable to Enlightenment ways of thinking and have resulted in the alleviation of much human suffering. Because of innovations made possible by these ways of thinking, we have to spend much less time doing back-breaking labor to survive and have more time for things such as studying the Bible. And the Enlightenment has resulted in positive developments regarding how the Bible itself is read and understood. The emphasis on reason means that persons no longer feel themselves dependent on those in authority in the church to tell them what the Bible says or means. As we will discuss in the next chapter, new ways of reading and interpreting the Bible developed that helped free the Bible from the dogmatic interpretations of it by those in authority in churches.

At the same time, the Enlightenment and modern culture also created complications and difficulties for reading and interpreting the Bible. First, although it should be obvious, those who wrote the Bible did not view the world in the ways those of us shaped by the Enlightenment view it. The people who lived in biblical times and wrote the material we now have in our Bible did not understand "reason" in any way as those in the Enlightenment did. They knew nothing of science as we understand science. They did not perceive that "truth" was tied to facts or that for something to be true it had to be verifiable. The Bible emerged in a world that was culturally far removed from the modern world. If we are to understand and appreciate the Bible, we must recognize that it participates in a different cultural world from ours.

Second, because of the Enlightenment, new ways of reading and interpreting the Bible developed. Before the Enlightenment, it was assumed that the Bible was "true" and could be taken literally. What the Bible said happened was assumed to have happened. In a similar vein, the doctrines or dogmas of the church were also accepted as "true" and were not often challenged. With the Enlightenment, both the Bible and the authoritative pronouncements of the church were subject to the scrutiny of reason. The Bible says that God created the world in six days (Genesis 1) and that Jesus turned water into wine (Jn. 2:1–11), but reason and scientific analysis cannot confirm such claims as factually true or scientifically likely.

Marcus Borg makes this keen observation about the impact of the modern concern with "facts" on interpreting the Bible in particular and on Christianity more generally:

> The modern preoccupation with factuality has had a pervasive and distorting effect on how we see the Bible and Christianity. During most of the nineteenth and twentieth centuries, many Christians and much of Christian theology were caught between the two sterile choices of literalism… and reductionism. The first sought to defend the factual accuracy and uniqueness of the Bible and Christianity. The second tended to reduce the Bible and Christianity to what made sense within the modern worldview. Both are thoroughly modern positions.[19]

Because we teach the Bible in churches that are very much a part of Western culture, we will find many persons who believe their choices are those identified by Borg. When we recognize that the Bible does not share our modern assumptions, we can then see that it is not appropriate to do with the Bible what Borg identifies has been done so often in the last two centuries: either defend the factual accuracy of the Bible or reduce the Bible to make sense in our modern worldview. These options are efforts to fit a square peg into a round hole. They fail to perceive the differences between modernity and the biblical world and in turn attempt to force our modern cultural assumptions onto texts that reflect ancient cultural assumptions.

In terms of intercultural education, these responses to the cultural differences between modernity and the Bible identified by Borg are expressions of denial and defense. They also tend to minimize the cultural distance between the modern world and the biblical world. In the next chapter, which is concerned with biblical interpretation, we make a case for interpretative possibilities that move beyond these two options.

Before turning to other expressions of contemporary culture, it is necessary to discuss one more issue regarding Western culture or modernity. In recent years there have been challenges to the assumptions of modernity. It is common to hear that we are now living in a postmodern culture. This claim suggests that a new cultural paradigm—new ways of living, thinking, and valuing—is beginning to emerge (some would say it has already emerged). This new cultural paradigm makes assumptions that challenge the way Western culture, with its Enlightenment grounding, perceives the world. Marcus Borg is again helpful in summarizing the characteristics of postmodernity:

1. First, postmodernity is marked by the realization that modernity itself is a culturally conditioned, relative historical construction. The modern worldview is not the final word about reality any more than previous worldviews have been.

2. Second, postmodernity is marked by a turn to experience. In a time when traditional religious teachings have become suspect, we tend to trust that which can be known in our own experience. This turn to experience is seen in the remarkable resurgence of interest in spirituality within mainline churches and beyond.

3. Third, postmodernity is marked by a movement beyond fact fundamentalism to the realization that stories can be true without being literally and factually true...An obvious point that has often been forgotten during the period of modernity: Metaphors and metaphorical narratives can be profoundly true even if they are not literally or factually true.[20]

The contours of this emerging "postmodern" culture described by Borg are not yet fully clear. In some ways the assumptions of postmodern culture, particularly the understanding that claims can be true though not factual (Borg's third point above), reflect a more biblical perspective and hold promise for biblical interpreters and teachers. Yet there are also aspects of this emerging postmodern culture that are quite problematic for interpreting and teaching the Bible. No aspect of postmodernism is more difficult for this task than its denial of any transcendence and its pervasive sense of relativism.[21] As postmodern culture takes clearer form, we will need to become students of it and the new challenges it will present for intercultural engagement with the Bible.

The Culture of the United States (American Culture)[22]

Modern and postmodern cultures exercise a dominant influence in the United States. However, it is possible to identify a culture that is more specific to the United States and is shaped by the uniqueness of the American setting and experiences. Persons who study the Bible in the United States are influenced not only by modern and postmodern cultures but also by the unique culture of the United States, by an American culture.[23] Like modern and postmodern cultures, the culture of the United States is a complex phenomenon. In this discussion we draw on the description of American culture offered by William Dyrness in his book *How Does America Hear the Gospel?*[24]

Dyrness argues that there is conflict between the culture of the United States and the Christian gospel, particularly in the realm of values.[25] We largely agree with Dyrness's argument, though he has a broader concern than ours. We are interested in Dyrness's analysis because we understand that in churches in the United States, persons will come to the study of the Bible having been deeply shaped by the phenomena of American culture that Dyrness describes. Unless we who teach and study the Bible in our country's setting are aware of the American culture that powerfully shapes the way we live and think and perceive reality, we will be unable to engage seriously the Bible and its cultures, which are quite different from American culture. As intercultural educators warn us, if we are not aware of our own culture, we will deny and minimize cultural differences. Even worse, we will be tempted to defend our American culture against biblical cultures that we perceive to be not only different but inferior and wrong. Such defensiveness provides an excuse not to take the Bible seriously and gives persons permission to dismiss biblical claims.

Dyrness's description of the culture of the United States has three foci, which he labels as "The Virgin Land," "The American Dream," and "The American Adam." In speaking of the "Virgin Land," Dyrness describes elements of the culture of the United States that have been shaped by the country's geographic setting and the resulting sense that the United States is a land of unlimited potential and growth.[26] Among the significant observations about the land and its meaning for American culture identified by Dyrness are these: (1) God sent settlers to this place; (2) westward expansion has shown the land to be boundless (Manifest Destiny); (3) the land is connected to ideals and visions of what it means to be human; that is, persons are created to work the land, and in working the land there is purity of character and integrity; and (4) the land supports unlimited growth and potential, a view that leads to a "pragmatic materialism," or the sense that the land exists to serve our ends. Thus Dyrness proposes that from the experience of the land a sense of the culture emerges.[27] There is freedom to move with no limitations, and in moving there is progress. There is the need to move quickly, to hurry, because there is a lot to do and a long way to go; things are there to acquire, use up, and throw away.

In speaking of "The American Dream," Dyrness explores the sense that America is the land where all things are possible.[28] Among the significant observations made by Dyrness about the American dream are the following: (1) the idea that all things are possible derives from a sense that America is the new Israel and the firstfruits of the fulfillment of God's eschatological purposes, thus creating an "ethos of privilege"[29]; (2) from America's sense of being a special place comes a sense of special responsibility, that we must do better; and (3) there is in America a sense that all problems can be solved and everything is possible. Dyrness asserts that from this sense that all things are possible, a particular view of life is widely held in the United States. This is the view that there is unlimited potential to overcome and leave behind the problems of the past and to create a better future, a view of life Dyrness calls "temporal optimism."[30]

Finally, in speaking of "The American Adam," Dyrness describes the American idea that all persons can fulfill their potential.[31] Dyrness asserts that the sense of America as a people living in a land of unlimited growth and potential where all things are possible focuses especially on the individual. He believes this focus is influenced by several factors. Religiously, the Puritans introduced this emphasis with their valuing of individual religious experience, for example, the Great Awakening. Philosophically, America has affirmed the Enlightenment view that reason sets persons free from the tyranny of authority. Politically influenced by the work of John Locke, the basis of society in the United States has been seen as a social contract between the individual and society to which individuals need to agree. And drawing on Adam Smith, it has often been understood that economic well-being could be achieved when every person acted in his or her own self-interest. Dyrness indicates that during the 1800s, the biblical Adam became the symbol for what it meant to be an American: "The American was the new Adam striding across Eden with the innocence and vitality of youth."[32] The American cultural sense that all persons can fulfill their potential finds contemporary expression in the psychologies of self-actualization from writers such as Abraham Maslow and Thomas Harris (*I'm OK—You're OK*).

For most citizens of the United States, including Christians, the cultural values Dyrness identifies are taken for granted and assumed to be normative. Even more than normative, many American Christians think that the values and ideas Dyrness identifies as derived from particular American experiences are actually biblical values and ideas. As Dyrness frequently reminds his readers, the story of the United States has from its earliest beginnings been told using biblical images (seeing the United States as the "promised land" is an example).

It is quite easy to deny or minimize the significant differences between American culture and ideas and biblical cultures and ideas to the point where the two are conflated and hopelessly confused. Yet reflection on some of the American values identified by Dyrness quickly suggests significant tension with the Bible. Dyrness, for instance, suggests the tensions between the American sense of optimism and the themes of suffering that are closely tied to biblical notions about hope and salvation,[33] or the biblical concern for community, for "we," versus the near obsession of American culture with the individual, "I."[34] Our concern is that in teaching the Bible, it is crucial that we be keenly aware of the culture of the United States so we can recognize the ways it both complements and is in tension with the cultures of the Bible. Only with such awareness will we be able to help persons encounter the Bible on its own grounds and engage in a serious and transformative intercultural dialogue.

Church Cultures

In addition to Western culture and the culture of the United States, there are also church cultures that impact how the Bible is read and interpreted. When teaching the Bible, we need to take account of the church culture in which we are participating. It can be argued that each denomination, and, for that matter, each local congregation, has a unique culture—ways of living inclusive of values, beliefs, and so on. It is beyond the scope of this book to describe the cultures of particular denominations or congregations, though we want to alert those who teach the Bible in churches of the need to do so.[35] Instead, we offer a summary of a model for understanding American Protestant church cultures that we have found particularly helpful because it focuses on the impact of these cultures on how the Bible is read and interpreted. Again, we urge that persons teaching the Bible in churches develop an understanding of the culture of the particular denomination and congregation in which they are teaching.

Richard J. Mouw, in an article titled "The Bible in Twentieth-Century Protestantism: A Preliminary Taxonomy," attempts to address the question "How has the Bible been viewed by North American Protestants in the twentieth century? To be specific, how have they used the Bible? How have they appropriated its content?"[36] Mouw proposes four models by which this happens, four "minds at work," as Mouw calls it.[37]

1. The first way of thinking about the Bible that Mouw identifies he calls "doctrinalism." Those who hold this position "consider doctrine to be of fundamental importance" and see the Bible "as being primarily a source for doctrine."[38] Those who view the Bible in this way use scripture to develop doctrines, for instance, of God, Christ, humanity, church, and so on.

2. Another "mind at work" in American Protestantism is "pietism," Mouw says. What pietists value are "certain pious ('godly' or 'spiritual') experiences and habits" that they consider fundamental to Christian life; they react against doctrinalism, which they view as "dead orthodoxy" or a "purely intellectual" form of Christianity.[39] For pietists, the Bible is viewed as a "handbook for pious living" and as "crucial to fostering a personal sense of divine presence."[40] A good deal of popular devotional literature, such as *The Upper Room,* reflects this understanding of the Bible.

3. Mouw labels a third view of the Bible as "moralism." Stressing "moral or ethical categories," this "mind at work" views Christianity as "a system which helps human beings live the good life; it enables them to engage in right action."[41] Mouw recognizes that a moralistic view of Christianity can defend a range of positions—from strict prohibitions against drinking and smoking to strong commitment to Christian pacifism. The Bible is viewed "as a source book for moral principles or rules. Biblical morality, in this view, curbs our sinful tendencies."[42]

4. Finally, Mouw calls a fourth view of the Bible in American Protestantism "culturalism," in which "the Christian life is viewed in terms of the Christian's involvements in broad institutions of society"—politics, the economy, the arts, education, and so on.[43] This view of the Bible understands that Christians are called to participate in the institutional patterns of society. The Bible "becomes a book addressing primarily questions of culture."[44] As an example, Mouw cites Jim Wallis, the longtime editor of *Sojourners* magazine:

> The biblical witness presents a sharp contrast between "this world," dominated by principalities and powers, and the in breaking of the kingdom of God into human history which breaks the uncontested rule and domination of the powers.[45]

The goal of the Christian life is understood to be either imposing Christian patterns on the larger community or establishing alternative Christian organizations within the larger society.[46]

In describing these four ways of regarding the Bible, Mouw provides a perspective on the cultures of American Protestant churches—ways that churches think about and value the Bible and imagine their purposes as communities of faith. The implications of Mouw's models for teaching the Bible in the church need to be developed in two different directions.

First, we need to think of the four cultural models in relationship to the Bible itself. It is likely that at least parts of the Bible were written for all four of the purposes Mouw identifies. That is, there are biblical texts concerned with right behavior (moralism)—the Ten Commandments, portions of the Sermon on the Mount, or the admonitions that Paul often includes in his epistles. Other biblical texts are concerned with eliciting a heartfelt response to God (pietism)—for example, many of the psalms. At least a few biblical texts seem to have as their purpose to admonish correct doctrine (doctrinalism)—for instance, the letters of Timothy and Titus, at least in part. Finally, portions of scripture are concerned with how communities of faith relate to society (culturalism)—the most obvious concern of many of the prophetic books.

One can make a case that within the Bible itself one can find at least some texts whose purpose is consistent with all four models described by Mouw. The difficulty comes when we attempt to impose one model on all biblical texts. To do so is to deny the cultural differences between our contemporary setting (where, for example, the culture of our congregation may favor a pietist reading of the Bible with concern for a heartfelt experience of God) and the culture of a biblical text (where, for example, a text from the prophet Amos concerned with economic justice is better understood from the perspective of moralism or culturalism). In this way, denominational or congregational cultures become defensive and closed to a rich intercultural encounter with the Bible.

Second, we need to think about how Mouw's four models impact the dynamic of the church settings where we teach the Bible. A given congregation probably holds as dominant one of the positions described by Mouw. However, it is likely that all four cultures could be found in that congregation. When we are teaching the Bible, the dominant position of the congregation—that is, its culture—will impact how the Bible is read and interpreted. If there are conflicting biblical interpretations in that setting, it is likely that these conflicts are rooted in different understandings of the character and purpose of the Bible. Moralists, doctrinalists, pietists, and culturalists read biblical texts through different lenses and understand the significance of texts in different ways. Mouw's insights into the four cultural models of American Protestant churches help explain why there is likely to be conflict about biblical interpretations in settings where we teach. We are dealing with a cultural conflict that calls for intercultural education—developing an awareness of the cultural differences that persons bring to biblical texts and an appreciation and respect for those differences.

The Cultures of the Bible

We have considered the contemporary cultural contexts in which teaching the Bible occurs. Now we need to consider the cultures that were the context in which biblical literature was shaped. Remember that the premise of this chapter is that to engage scripture is a process of intercultural education. Those of us who study the Bible live in a complex web of contemporary cultures. That complexity is compounded by encountering scripture that reflects cultures very different from our contemporary ones.

The novelist Leslie Hartley begins his book *The Go-Between* with this line: "The past is a foreign country. They do things differently there."[47] Leading a class concerned with the cultures of scripture, we began by having the students remember and share about the strangest[48] place they had ever visited (such as the experience in Zaire Karen describes in the opening vignette of this chapter). When we study the Bible, we need always to keep in mind that we are visiting a very strange land, a foreign culture, a place where they do things differently.

Failure to recognize the cultural distance and difference at which we live from the Bible can result in misunderstandings and distortions of biblical texts, even texts whose sense seems quite clear. For instance, consider the familiar injunction from the book of Deuteronomy: "You shall love the LORD your God with all your heart, and with all your soul, and with all your might" (Deut. 6:5). Almost every word of this familiar passage is open to misunderstanding if we are not aware that it reflects ideas from a different culture.

To illustrate, our culture primarily associates "love" with romantic or erotic love. We consider love as something that happens to people—they "fall in love." This passage, using "love" as a command, likely has its background in notions of covenant loyalty and obligation that were common in the ancient Near Eastern world when Deuteronomy was written, around 600 B.C.E. "Love" is something that a vassal has an obligation to do toward an overlord, and emotions or feelings have nothing to do with this kind of "love." Further, our culture associates "heart" with feelings or affect ("That broke my heart!"). In the culture of the Old Testament, "heart" has to do with human will or intention. The Old Testament associates emotions with the kidneys or bowels! And finally, our culture often thinks of "soul" out of Greek cultural understandings, an inner part of us that survives death. In the Old Testament, "soul" is a way of referring to all that one is, such as we mean when we refer to ourselves with the pronoun "I." The point is, the Bible grows out of cultures that are very different from the Western and American cultures that so significantly shape how we think, value, and act. A serious engagement of scripture always involves an intercultural process.

When considering biblical cultures, it is important to remember that the Bible developed over a very long time—at least more than 1200 years from the earliest Old Testament material to the latest New Testament material. Written over this long expanse of history, many and diverse cultural influences are reflected in this book. We also need to remember that although biblical writings are largely the product of the area we know as Palestine, in both the Old and New Testament eras this region was heavily affected by cultural influences from a broader geographic sphere. In the Old Testament era there was a broad culture—a way of living, a language family, patterns of thinking, and so on—identified with the ancient Near East. However, particular cultural influences from Assyria, Egypt, Babylon, and Persia also impacted those who shaped the Old Testament. The New Testament was shaped by the pervasive influence of Roman culture and, in turn, Greek culture that heavily impacted Rome. Thus when we turn to the Bible, we need to be aware of the influence of many ancient cultures. There is not *a* biblical culture, but *many* biblical cultures.

Because of the complexity of cultures and the Bible, a comprehensive discussion of this topic is not possible within the scope of this book. Instead, let's look at an example of the cultural distance and difference between biblical cultures and the contemporary cultures in which we participate in order to further raise our awareness of the cultural complexity that exists when we study scripture. When we discussed Western and American cultures, a prominent feature of both was the importance of the individual. Our contemporary cultural context stresses individuality, the individual person set free to discover truth through reason, to participate in the American dream, in which all things are possible. Rugged individualism is an important ideal in the United States, an ideal, for instance, that is reflected in activities from economics (self-made persons who have pulled themselves up by their bootstraps) to education (we honor the outstanding students who have excelled above the crowd) to athletics (we want athletic heroes who single-handedly take over a game and achieve victory) to the arts (we recognize the outstanding artists whose accomplishments set them apart in their field). Individualism is a central value of contemporary culture.

In both the Old and New Testaments, despite nuances of difference in different biblical literatures, it must be said that there does not exist any sense of the individual as we think of it. Instead, in the ancient cultures reflected in the Bible there is much more a corporate sense of who a person is. As we mentioned earlier in this chapter, when in our culture we hear someone say "you," we hear that as an address to a single individual; we hear "me." However, in the ancient cultures reflected in the Bible, the dominant way in which "you" was understood was plural, an address not to an individual but to a community.

Hans Walter Wolff, a German Old Testament scholar, has noted of the individual in the Old Testament:

The life of the individual in ancient Israel is always firmly integrated in the bonds of his [sic] family and thus of his people. Wherever he is set apart or isolated, something unusual, if not something threatening, is happening.[49]

For those of us living in the twenty-first century, a community is composed of individuals who choose to join it. Our notion of community and society comes from Enlightenment philosophers such as John Locke, important to the founders of the United States, who spoke of the formation of a society as a process of persons choosing to enter a "social contract." As Wolff indicates, ancient Israel's understanding of the relationship between community or society and individuals turns our cultural understanding on its head. The community comes first, and individual persons cannot be understood apart from the social group—family, clan, tribe, or national grouping—of which they are a part.

Reflecting on this way of seeing the relationship between society and the individual, another Old Testament scholar observed the following:

> In Israelite social organisation the group was more important than the individual, with the result that a group could be held responsible and punished for a misdeed of one of its members, as when Achan's family was put to death because Achan had kept for himself some spoil from Jericho (Joshua 7:24–26). But this seemingly crude method of carrying out justice was itself only an example of a fundamentally different way in which Israelites classified and encountered the world around them.[50]

The cultural understanding of the relationship between the individual and society in the Old Testament certainly seems odd to those of us living in a cultural context that understands that the individual precedes the society. Yet as noted in the quotation above, the way that Israel understands the relationship between the individual and society is "only an example of a fundamentally different way in which Israelites classified and encountered the world around them."

Much of what has been said about the Old Testament cultures' understanding of the relationship between the individual and society is also evident in the New Testament. After citing numerous texts from New Testament letters concerned with the realization of God's intention for humanity through Christ (e.g., Rom. 8:17, 29; 1 Cor.

15:49; Col. 1:15, 3:10), George Ernest Wright, a twentieth-century biblical scholar, makes this claim:

> Yet the new and responsible individual who is created by God in Christ is not liberated from community in such a manner as would enable us to speak of biblical faith as creating a true individualism over against all collectivism. Man [*sic*] is here liberated from a false to a true sense of community, and for that reason his [*sic*] first steps in the right direction are to be discovered in conversion. While in modern times we see a rediscovery of community which enslaves man, so that collectivism and individualism appear as opposing concepts, the biblical concentration of attention on God's formation of a people is of such a nature that man [*sic*], the individual, emerges in society in a manner hitherto unknown. The biblical story must not be interpreted as the progressive emancipation of the individual, but instead as God's action in history to create a community in which the responsible individual finds his [*sic*] true being.[51]

In our contemporary cultural setting, we tend to think of the transformation effected by God through Christ as changing each of us individually. In its extreme form, many contemporary Christians have an individualistic view of salvation. God saves each person one at a time. Wright argues that in the cultural context of the New Testament there is a different understanding of human transformation. Through Jesus Christ God creates a new community in relationship to which persons realize their full humanity. Thus, pervasively in the gospels Jesus invites people to participate in the coming reign of God; at Pentecost persons are baptized and become part of a new community that holds all things in common (Acts 2); and Paul thinks of the church as the body of Christ to which Christians belong as members (1 Cor. 12; compare Ephesians 4).

Although we have examined the different understandings of the relationship between individuals and communities present in biblical cultures (communities define individuals) and in our contemporary culture (communities are defined by the individuals who comprise them), we do not want this illustration to obscure the larger point we are attempting to make. The Bible reflects cultural settings that are significantly different from the cultural settings in which we participate. No matter where we turn in scripture, we need to be aware that biblical texts are grounded in cultures very different from our own.

Whenever we engage the Bible, we are involved in a cross-cultural encounter just as surely as if we got on a plane and flew halfway around the world to visit a distant land. The worlds of the Old and New Testaments are culturally quite different from the cultures in which we are immersed daily. When encountering these worlds, most of us and those whom we are teaching will experience "the annoyance of being lost." If we are to teach in ways that help persons see and understand the world from the perspective of the biblical texts, we will need to teach in order to develop intercultural competence, the ability to be aware of and move within both our own cultural context and the cultural worlds of the Bible. When we teach the Bible in the church, we must remember that we are engaged in an intercultural education process that calls for the kinds of awareness and skills we have introduced in this chapter.

Summary and Implications for Teaching the Bible

Teaching the Bible is an intercultural education experience. It is an experience that calls us to become aware of the cultural perspectives we bring to the reading of texts, to become aware of those cultures out of which the texts themselves come, and to develop the ability to engage these various layers of culture in ways that help us to draw insight and meaning from the Bible in order to give shape to and transform our lives as Christians. Given the intercultural nature of teaching the Bible that we have described in this chapter, what are some important implications for teaching the Bible in the church that we might name? Although certainly not exhaustive of the insights we might draw from our discussion of intercultural education, we want to name four basic principles that we feel are vital guides to our teaching.

1. *Remember that we are all cultural beings.* It is such an obvious fact but bears our saying it loud and clear again. We are all culturally embedded creatures—those of us reading the Bible in the twenty-first century and those writing it centuries ago. Remembering that we are all shaped by culture is the first step in naming and claiming

the cultural lenses through which we read the biblical text and acknowledging the different lenses from which the text emerged. For teachers of the Bible, it is the first step in taking the cultural nature of our task seriously in order that we can help our students and ourselves move toward intercultural competence as we study scripture.

2. *Teach for cultural awareness.* Teaching for awareness is key in intercultural education. When teaching the Bible, we need to help our students become aware of their own cultural lenses, that "ocean" within which they swim and how it influences the way they read the text. We need to help our students become aware of the cultures of the Bible and be able to acknowledge that these cultures are indeed unique and not like ours. Too often a lack of awareness of both our own and others' culture leads to that false assumption of cultural similarity that is a mark of minimalization. Such an assumption risks both a misreading and misinterpretation of the text and limits the opportunity to find authentic meaning that can inform and transform.

3. *Teach for cultural appreciation and respect.* It is not enough to just teach for awareness of cultural perspectives. It is also important that we teach for appreciation and respect. This includes helping our students name, appreciate, and respect those cultural traits that are basic to who they are. We gain nothing by belittling our own cultural context in order to value another. At the same time, however, we also need to admit that our way of perceiving the world is not universal and that others might have something to teach us. Coming to the Bible with an openness to respect the cultures we find reflected there and to appreciate that we can learn something from them is a vital part of engaging the text. As teachers of the Bible, we will take time to help our students come to know the cultures they encounter and to appreciate and respect them.

4. *Teach for intercultural competence.* Intercultural competence is the ability to move among cultures in ways that lead us to learn and to grow from the encounters. It is a process that moves us from denial, defense, and minimization to acceptance of the other culture, to adaptation or empathetic engagement of the culture, and finally to integration, in which we find ourselves able to be "at home" in both. It involves developing the kinds of awareness, appreciation, and

respect of which we've spoken. As teachers of the Bible, it is both a challenge and a responsibility to teach toward such competence, trusting that such competence leads to the kind of transformative engagement with scripture that we seek for our students and ourselves.

4

Teaching the Bible: Issues of Interpretation

Imagine this scene: It is the initial gathering of a newly formed women's evening Bible study. Pastor Mary has decided to begin with a study of the book of Genesis. After an opening devotion and introductions, she reads aloud the creation story in Genesis 1. She then invites the women to share their responses to this familiar text. Even though the group is new, responses come quickly:

Alice indicates that she finds it reassuring that God is so powerful that in just seven days He was able to create everything in the world just like it is. Martha quickly agrees, though she asks if Pastor Mary thinks when the text talks about a "day" it was the same length day as we now know.

Maureen says she likes this version of the creation better than the one in Genesis 2, but wants to know if Pastor Mary will talk about why there are two creation stories back-to-back in Genesis 1 and 2. "Were these stories written by different authors at different times?" she asks.

Susan notes that in hearing the story read aloud, she heard in fresh ways the beauty of the repetitions in the text: "And God said...God saw that it was good...And there was evening and there was morning..." She wonders aloud how these repetitions might be important to what the text is saying.

Joyce's voice is firm as she says that she did not much appreciate this story because she heard God's command to "have dominion" as giving permission to abuse the environment. However, she adds with some sarcasm, it could have been worse. They could be studying Genesis 2, which presents women as subordinate "helpers" of men.

From our experience of teaching the Bible in churches, the above exchange is typical of what happens when persons begin to engage biblical texts. They respond in a wide variety of ways, ways that reflect unacknowledged but deeply held assumptions about how biblical texts are to be interpreted.

Intentional interpretation is important when teaching the Bible in churches. Those who teach the Bible, if they are to teach responsibly and intentionally, need to be self-aware of the ways that they are interpreting biblical texts as they teach.[1] Further, having an awareness of the basic ways biblical texts are interpreted can help teachers understand how students are approaching and understanding biblical texts. Such insight allows teachers to help their students understand the ways they already interpret and understand biblical texts. Such insight also allows teachers a perspective from which to challenge students to explore new ways of interpreting and understanding the Bible. Finally, persons who teach with self-awareness about interpretative approaches can help their students also become intentional, self-aware, and responsible interpreters of biblical texts.

In this chapter a model is presented for understanding the most common ways that the Bible is interpreted. These different ways of interpreting the Bible are then discussed and illustrated. As different ways of reading and interpreting the Bible are presented, we offer suggestions about the ways each approach may be used in teaching the Bible in the church.

Intentional Ways of Reading the Bible

At the outset it must be recognized that there are many different types of writings in the Bible. The women in the Bible study described at the beginning of this chapter may have responded differently if their pastor had read, instead of Genesis 1, a psalm, a portion of the Sermon on the Mount, or a section from one of Paul's letters. Different kinds of biblical writings lend themselves more to one way of reading and interpreting than another. Nonetheless, the different ways that the women from the newly formed evening Bible study understood Genesis 1 reflect important ways that persons over the last two centuries in Western culture have read and understood the meaning of texts—biblical texts, to be sure, but not just biblical texts. The skills used to read and understand the meaning of the Bible are closely related to the skills we use to read and understand the meaning of all kinds of material that we encounter every day.

The basic ways of reading and interpreting biblical texts are reflected in this chart:

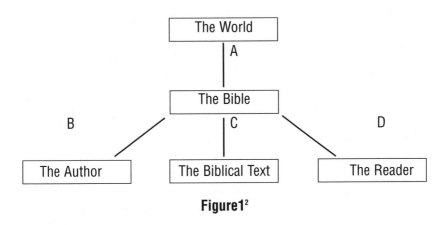

Figure1[2]

There are four primary ways that biblical texts can be read and understood:

1. As a text reflects or describes the world (Line A)

2. As a text relates to its author and the circumstances of the author (line B)

3. As the biblical text itself is the focus of interpretation—its literary features, its artistry, the ways it makes its point (line C)

4. As the text relates to its contemporary readers—who they are, what they value, and what they bring to their reading of the text (line D)

The response of the women to Genesis 1 reflect these four ways of reading and making sense of biblical texts. Each of us, consciously or not, uses one or more of these ways of reading texts. We will outline briefly what is involved with each interpretative approach and indicate some implications of each approach for teaching the Bible in the church.

A Text Describes the World

A text can be understood to reflect or describe the world. In figure 1, this interpretative approach is represented by Line A, which connects the "Bible" box in the center of the chart to the "World" box at the top of the chart. This is the way that Alice understands Genesis 1. For Alice, Genesis 1 is to be taken at face value, as a text that describes what happened long ago when the world began at God's command. Alice assumes that the text is literally "true"; that is, it presents a factually accurate description of the world. Martha understands the story much like Alice except that she does not think every detail of the story needs to be taken literally. She wonders if a "day" might have meant something different from what we now understand. Alice, and to a lesser extent Martha, understand Genesis 1 to be *literally and factually true.*

When a text is read in this way, it is assumed that a text is to be taken literally; that is, that a text presents a factual account of that which it describes (if the text is a narrative). Although we have been using Genesis 1 as an illustration, the same principle can apply to other texts. Thus, those who read biblical texts assuming that they reflect the way the world is would read material from one of the gospels—for instance, Matthew's story of Jesus' birth—and assume that it is a factual account. Because there are differing accounts of the creation (in Genesis 1 and 2) and of Jesus' birth (in Matthew and Luke), those who read biblical texts assuming they are factual reports often find it necessary to harmonize these accounts. That is, they assume the differing accounts of the same event are complementary, can be fitted together, and so weave differing accounts into one blended story. Often, Christmas pageants are examples of such harmonizing—the shepherds and angel choir from Luke's gospel, the magi from Matthew, and so on.

It needs to be said that for most of the history of the church, the Bible has been read and understood more or less literally. Such literal interpretations of the Bible began to be questioned because of developments in Western culture, particularly the Enlightenment.[3] Nonetheless, today there are still many people like Alice in our churches who read the Bible in the literal and factual way described here.

One reason that persons read the Bible literally is their assumptions about what it means that the Bible is the word of God. Many people assume the claim "the Bible is God's Word" means that God is in some direct way the author of the Bible—God wrote it directly, or at least God directed the humans who wrote down what God intended.[4] There are, however, other ways of thinking about authorship of the Bible and the Bible as the word of God. Our own assumption is that the Bible was written by humans who were reflecting on their experiences of God in the concrete, historical circumstances of their life. Their writings—our Bible—bear witness to the ways they experienced God. Over time, communities of faithful people—Israel and the church—have accepted these writings as faithful witnesses to who God is and what God is about in the world. Indeed, these books, written by humans, are recognized as a means by which we, too, can experience God.[5] We affirm the Bible to be the word of God, but not because God is directly the author of the Bible or because it is literally and factually true. Although we recognize why some people read the Bible literally and factually, we do not share those assumptions as we think about teaching the Bible in the church.

The inclination of Western culture to want objective facts or data is another reason that many people read the Bible factually (see chapter 3). We want to know the facts, what happened, and so our assumption is that the Bible reflects our Western interest in these. When we read the Bible, our cultural bias leads us to assume that it provides "objective reports" about the events it narrates, much like a history book or our morning newspapers. We indicated in the prior chapter, however, that for the people in the cultures in which the Bible was shaped, there was little understanding of or interest in what we in our culture call objective or factual reports. Instead, those who wrote the Bible had a primary interest in recounting their experiences of God, in writing from what we call a confessional perspective.[6]

For many centuries persons have questioned if the Bible should be read literally. Since the mid-1800s, however, under the influence of the Enlightenment, many churches have increasingly understood that to read the Bible literally, as a factual description of what happened long ago, is not possible. This is not to deny that behind the stories of the Old and New Testaments something happened: slaves escaped Egypt; Israel was ruled by King David; Jesus lived, taught, was crucified, and was experienced by his followers as risen, alive once more; the church grew in the Mediterranean world and began to include Gentiles. The issue is not if something happened, but rather how biblical texts are related to what happened. We understand that biblical texts are not so much "factual reports" of events as they are confessions of faith about the ways persons experienced God. Thus:

- The meaning of Genesis 1 is not in that it "describes" how the world began, but rather in the claim it makes about the sovereignty of God over the world, however it came to be.

- The meaning of the exodus story is not in that it factually "describes" how some slaves escaped from Egypt, but rather in the claim it makes about God's concern that marginalized and oppressed peoples be set free for new life.

- The meaning of Matthew's story of Jesus is not in that it factually describes the events of Jesus' life, but rather in the claim that, in Jesus, God was with us (the name "Emmanuel" in the birth story in Matthew 1) and continues to be with us (the commission to the disciples in Matthew 28).

- The meaning of Paul's letters to the church in Corinth is not that they offer us "factual" information about that church, but rather that Paul's letters raise important concerns about what it means to be the church today.

Such understandings of the nature and character of the Bible shape our approach to teaching the Bible in the church.

Still, all of us who teach the Bible in churches must recognize that there are many people, like Alice, who do interpret the Bible as literally and factually "true." These persons love the Lord and are devoted disciples of Jesus. We have an obligation, as teachers of the church, to treat the many persons like Alice with respect. We need to be careful to question their deeply held beliefs gently, and when we do question the deeply held beliefs of persons like Alice, we need to be prepared to spend time helping them think through new ways of viewing the Bible.

In this chapter we will talk about ways that we might attempt to engage persons who take the Bible literally. However, a literal reading of many biblical texts is no longer possible for many of us. If the Bible, or at least significant parts of the Bible, cannot readily be understood to reflect the world in some literal and factual manner, how else might the Bible be read and interpreted?

A Text Reflects Its Author

A biblical text can be understood to reflect its author, the circumstances being addressed by the author, and the author's audience. In figure 1, this way of reading and interpreting biblical texts is represented by line B, which connects the "Bible" box with the "Author" box. Maureen, noting the different versions of the creation in Genesis 1 and 2, inquired about the historical background of these two stories. She wanted to know who wrote each story and when. Her unstated assumption was that to know something about the author of a biblical text and the setting in which it was written is important to understanding the Bible's meaning. Maureen's inquiry links the meaning of the story to its author and the circumstances in which the story was written.

This way of interpreting biblical texts is often referred to as a historical-critical approach.[7] The historical background of a text—who wrote the text, under what circumstances, to what audience—is understood to be the key to understanding a text's meaning. Genesis 1 and 2 can be used to illustrate this approach. The creation stories in both Genesis 1 and Genesis 2 probably drew on existing stories that would have been widely known in the ancient Near Eastern world of which Israel was a part. However, the "borrowed" stories were reshaped to reflect Israel's understanding of God. The usual judgment of biblical scholars is that Genesis 2 was written and included as part of Israel's sacred texts before Genesis 1.

Genesis 2 is thought to have been written close to the time when David and Solomon were Israel's kings by a writer commonly referred to as the "Yahwist" (or sometimes the J Writer). This writer is associated with material found from Genesis through Numbers, and some argue that there are also stories by the Yahwist in Joshua. We do not actually know the writer's name, and it is likely that the Yahwist was not an individual but a group of writers. These writers are referred to as the Yahwist Writers because they refer to God as "Yahweh" (the proper name for God in the Old Testament, usually translated in English versions as "The LORD"—for example, see Gen. 2:4).[8] Scholars identify the stories attributed to the Yahwist Writers by the vocabulary they use, the style of their writing, and the overall point of view they present. If these scholars are correct, Genesis 2 would have stood as Israel's creation story for a long time—several hundred years—before the Genesis 1 version was developed.

Genesis 1 is thought to have been written sometime after the Babylonian exile of Judah that occurred in 587 B.C.E. The writers responsible for the Genesis 1 creation story are called the Priestly Writers (or P Writers) because they were concerned about rituals and worship. Like the Yahwist Writers, material is attributed to the Priestly Writers on the basis of the vocabulary they use, the style of their writing, and the overall point of view they present. These writers, too, had a significant role in shaping the books of Genesis through Numbers.

The Priestly Writers were attempting to address the tragedy of the Babylonian exile in 587 B.C.E that resulted in the destruction of Jerusalem and the Temple, the end of the Davidic monarchy, and the loss of the promised land. Judah's defeat by Babylon was much more than a political crisis; it also created a spiritual or theological crisis. It seemed to many who had experienced the exile that God was either powerless or uncaring, and it is this despair and loss of confidence in God that the Priestly Writers attempted to address.

Why did the Priestly Writers think that a "new" creation story was needed if there already was one in Genesis 2? It could be that they judged the existing creation story in Genesis 2 inadequate for the difficult situation they confronted. Notice how the Genesis 2 creation story talks about the condition of the world before God's creative activity began:

> In the day that the LORD God made the earth and the heavens, when no plant of the field was yet in the earth and no herb of the field had yet sprung up—for the LORD God had not caused it to rain upon the earth, and there was no one to till the ground. (Gen. 2:4–5)

As God's creative activity begins, the earth is imagined to be an untended garden needing water and a gardener. God provides the water and creates humankind to "till…and keep" the garden (Gen. 2:15).

Compare this to the way that Genesis 1 imagines the state of things before God's creative activity begins:

> The earth was a formless void and darkness covered the face of the deep, while a wind from God swept over the face of the waters. (Gen. 1:2)

Here, the language reflects the way people in the ancient Near Eastern world of which Israel was a part spoke of cosmic chaos. There is a dramatic difference in the ways that Genesis 1 and 2 describe the challenge God faces in bringing order to the world. In Genesis 2 the problem is much more manageable—a little water and a gardener will do it. We might imagine that the Yahwistic Writers had in mind how a king like David or Solomon could serve God's creation helpfully. In Genesis 1, however, the problem God faced is much more significant—the whole cosmos is in disarray. Why would the Priestly Writers begin their creation story with such a dramatic portrayal of the severity of chaos? It could well be they did so because they experienced life in the midst of the Babylonian exile as quite chaotic, chaotic in a way that the Genesis 2 creation story just did not capture. The circumstances of the Yahwistic Writers and the Priestly Writers were very, very different. The Yahwistic Writers lived in a time of optimism and confidence about what the newly established monarchy could do. The Priestly Writers lived in a time of despair brought about by the collapse of meaning caused by the Babylonian exile.

The point of comparing the ways that the creation stories in Genesis 1 and 2 begin is to illustrate how biblical texts can be interpreted by understanding them in relationship to their author, the circumstances in which they were written, and the audience that is being addressed. This historical-critical approach that we have illustrated with the Genesis creation stories can be used with many other texts as well.[9]

The book of Amos comes alive when one begins to understand the economic situation of Israel in the mid-eighth century B.C. It was a time of great affluence. Israel's affluence, however, was gained by the exploitative economic policies of the monarchy. Such exploitation contradicted the ethos of the God whom Israel encountered in the exodus from Egypt. Understanding the social setting of the prophet helps one understand the book of Amos and also to see parallels to our contemporary situation.

There are good reasons that Matthew and Luke tell the story of Jesus' birth differently. One reason may be that the gospel writers had access to different traditions about Jesus' birth. The most significant reason, however, that they tell the story differently is that they were addressing different congregations with different issues. Matthew's story, careful to connect Jesus with the Old Testament, shows concern for how Christians and Jews might relate. One suspects this was important in the church for whom Matthew wrote his gospel. Luke's story focuses on people on the margins—Mary and Joseph, who are forced to journey to Bethlehem by the Roman authorities, and shepherds, who were socially marginal people. One suspects that in Luke's church, issues about marginalized people were important. One is helped to understand the different emphases of the gospels if one understands something about the audiences for whom the different gospels were written.

When reading Paul's letters, it is very helpful to know something about the churches to whom Paul writes and their setting. For instance, when one knows that Corinth was a cosmopolitan center with a great diversity of people and also an important economic hub, then some of the conflicts that Paul must address make sense. Further, one can appreciate why Paul might use the banking metaphor of reconciliation (2 Cor. 4) to explain the work of God through Christ to the church in Corinth, but not elsewhere in his letters.

This historical-critical approach has been the dominant way that Western biblical scholars have interpreted biblical texts since the mid-1800s and the dominant way that most mainline Protestant church pastors have been educated to interpret the Bible. This approach is widely evident in Bible commentaries and resources and also informs many published educational resources.

There are many reasons to consider seriously this interpretative approach when teaching the Bible in churches. Perhaps most importantly, this approach challenges those in the church to think specifically about the ways that persons, in the concreteness of their historical circumstances, experienced God and offered testimony about that experience—by telling or retelling stories, by protesting the injustice of society, by offering a prayer, by writing a letter to give guidance, and so on. Then, having thought about the testimony of those who lived long ago, this approach invites those of us in the church today to ask about our own circumstances and experiences of God. How are we and our situations like and different from those reflected in biblical texts? How is our experience of God like and different from that to which the text bears witness? Viewed in such a way, a biblical text may become a mirror in which we find ourselves reflected. We may conclude that we are not so different from the Corinthians and should give heed to Paul's concern for lack of respect shown persons who were less affluent (1 Cor. 11:17–22). Or maybe, to our chagrin, we will discover in reading Amos that our society exploits the poor much as the ancient society that the prophet condemns did.

One of the strengths of this approach to interpreting the Bible for teaching in the church is that it offers rich opportunities to make connections, connections that are the essence of learning. If we are able to see the circumstances that led the author of a biblical text to reflect about God in ways that connect to our contemporary circumstances, then the relevance of a text's claims about God or about the mission of God's people, for instance, become almost transparent. Another strength of this interpretative approach is its sensitivity to intercultural issues. This historical-critical approach insists that we give attention to the cultural factors at play in biblical texts—the cultural assumptions of the text's author and the audience for whom the text was originally intended. At the same time, attention to the cultural assumptions that surround the biblical text stimulate awareness of the culture in which we who are studying a text live. Such cultural awareness, as we have discussed already, allows us to respect the integrity of the biblical text and its cultural assumptions. Such cultural awareness also provides us a perspective to perceive, understand, appreciate, and critique our own culture.

Even though this historical-critical approach is a rich resource for teaching the Bible in the church, some cautions are necessary. First, it needs to be acknowledged that those who choose this approach must be prepared to do their homework before teaching. It requires a good deal of preparation and likely some hard study for teachers to feel confident that they understand who the author of a biblical text was, the circumstances in which a text was written, and the audience for whom a text was intended. Although such information about biblical texts is readily available in many resources, it takes time and effort to find it and organize it for teaching.

Second, one must be aware of a particular pitfall when teaching from a historical-critical interpretative approach. The danger is that our teaching will become engrossed in providing information *about* the biblical text, and in so doing we will never get to the transformational purposes of Bible study. Care is needed at this point. We certainly want to affirm the importance of knowing some information about biblical texts in order to read and understand them. We believe it makes a difference if one knows that the Priestly Writers wrote Genesis 1 or what the city Corinth was like as a background for reading Paul's Corinthian correspondence. If, however, our teaching gets no further than a discussion of the Priestly Writers and their setting in the Babylonian exile or of the cosmopolitan culture of ancient Corinth, then we have failed to engage the Bible seriously. It is important to identify the historical background of the gospel of Matthew, but finally what needs to concern us about Matthew's story of Jesus is how we in the church today may be formed as Jesus' disciples by this story. As we stated in our introduction, we assume that teaching the Bible has as its goal not just the conveying of information, but an invitation to transformation, an encounter with "that Mystery we call God."[10]

Third, in choosing to use a historical-critical interpretative approach when teaching the Bible in the church, thought needs to be given to who the participants will be. Young children, for instance, will simply not have the conceptual ability or life experience to use this approach. By the time children are in fifth or sixth grade, they will begin to have the conceptual ability to begin to understand the Bible in its historical context. In fact, exploring some of the historical and cultural aspects of the Bible is usually fun for young people in the older elementary grades and into middle school. Still, it is not likely that the approach we are describing here can be fully used until persons are at least in high school.

The historical-critical approach is certainly appropriate to use with adults. However, care needs to be taken about the assumptions with which adults come to study the Bible. Many adults will find this approach exciting and challenging if used as part of a skillfully designed teaching session. Nonetheless, some adults will find this approach quite threatening, especially persons who are inclined to read biblical texts more literally. Alice, for instance, in the women's Bible study class, will likely become quite uncomfortable if Pastor Mary presses a historical-critical interpretative approach to Genesis 1 and may well "downshift" and be unable to engage in the class in a meaningful way. At the same time, others in the group will be challenged and find this approach stimulating. When using this approach, care must be taken with persons like Alice, and if persons like Alice are the majority of participants, another interpretative approach may be better.

Finally, although the historical-critical approach is widely used, it does have its limitations. There are some portions of the Bible—the psalms, for instance—for which it is difficult if not impossible to identify the author, the audience, or the historical circumstances being addressed. There are also portions of the Bible whose composition is a composite—the product of many writers in many different circumstances addressing many different audiences over a considerable span of time. This is the case with many stories in the first five books of the Old Testament and also most of the prophetic books. What finally concerns the church is not to sort out the complex of intertwined sources of biblical literature but to read biblical books as an opportunity to be encountered by God. Therefore, we turn to another interpretative approach that has different assumptions about how to read and understand biblical texts. Rather than focusing on the author of a text, this approach focuses on the text itself.

Focusing on the Text Itself

A biblical text can be understood by focusing on the text itself, its literary features, its artistry, the ways it makes its point. In figure 1, this way of reading and interpreting biblical texts is represented by line C, which connects the "Bible" box with the "Biblical Text" box. In the women's evening Bible study group, Susan, in hearing Genesis 1 read aloud, noted the repetitions in the text: "And God said...God saw that it was good...And there was evening and there was morning..." She wondered how these repetitions might be important to what the text was saying. What Susan sensed in hearing Genesis 1 read aloud is that *attention to the text itself* can be a key to understanding the meaning of a text.

This way of reading a text assumes that features of the text itself are the key to understanding its meaning. Depending on what kind of text one is reading (a poem, a story, an epistle, for instance) and on which details of the text one focuses, this kind of interpretation is called by various names: literary, rhetorical, narrative, canonical, and so on.[11] In any case, the focus is on the text itself. In approaching a biblical text in this way, the concern is not with who wrote the text, in what circumstances, and to what audience—concerns that look *behind* the text as the key to its meaning. Rather, with this approach the focus stays on the text itself, not the world behind the text but the *world of the text*.[12]

This interpretative approach can be illustrated if one can imagine curling up with a good novel on a stormy day. Pretty soon, one is engrossed in the book, perhaps set on a resort island. After a while, if one looks out a window, it is something of a surprise to see that it is gray, cool, and rainy, because through the book one had been transported to a warm, sunny, tropical beach. When we are engrossed in a novel, we don't usually ask if it is "true," true in the sense that the characters were actual persons or that the tropical island is at some precise location or that there is a beach with white sand just as the novelist describes it. Rather, we surrender ourselves to the story and allow ourselves to enter into it. We imagine ourselves on the beach; we come to like some characters in the story but not others; we identify with some persons in the story but find other characters quite odd. If we are concerned if the story is "true," it is not so much the factual accuracy of the story's details that concerns us so much as whether we can identify with the story in some way. Are the characters credible? Do they act like people we know or like ourselves? Does the story mirror our world or give us insight into ourselves and our world? Good stories, or good poems for that matter, draw us in and invite us to explore the world that their texts create. We can read biblical texts in the same way.

Before illustrating this approach to biblical texts, let us press the uniqueness of this approach a step further. In reading a good novel, we may not even know much about the author or the circumstances in which the novel was written. One can read a novel, find it enjoyable, even insightful about the human condition, and know nothing about the author or the circumstances in which the novel was written. A good novel can stand on its own. Still, it can be helpful to understanding a novel if one does know something of the author and the circumstances that gave rise to the novel. For instance, one can read John Steinbeck's *Grapes of Wrath* knowing little of Steinbeck or American history. Yet when one knows something of Steinbeck and the circumstances of migrant workers in the mid-twentieth century, *Grapes of Wrath* will likely be even more compelling. One can focus on a biblical text and understand its meaning as one is drawn into the world of the text itself. Of course, we do not always know who wrote a biblical text and in what circumstances. But when we do, it can be helpful to know also something about the author and the circumstances in which the text was written as a way to see with even greater depth the possible meanings of a biblical text. Thus the approach we are discussing here, which focuses on the text itself, and the prior approach we discussed, which understands that a text reflects its author, can sometimes be used together.

We will again use Genesis 1 as a starting point to illustrate this approach to biblical texts that focuses on the text itself. Susan perceptively noted that in Genesis 1 there is a nearly identical pattern by which the creation of each day is recited:

And God said, "Let there be..." So God [made/created...][13] and separated...[14] God called...God saw that is was good. And there was evening and there was morning...day.

We might note some of the impact of this repeated pattern. For instance, this repeated pattern underscores that God is the sole actor in the drama, the subject of the verbs. Further, whatever God wills and commands comes into being. Thus, the repeated pattern of Genesis 1 emphasizes the utter sovereignty of God. Finally, the repeated pattern of this creation story leaves no doubt about how "good" God's creation is.

As we focus on the repeated pattern of the text for each day, day six attracts particular attention. It begins as the other days did, as the same pattern is used that is evident in the first five days. At verse 25, however, the pattern is broken. After the creation of the beasts of the land, where we expect the affirmation that there was evening and morning a sixth day, the phrase is missing. Instead, verse 26 announces further creative activity on the sixth day, the creation of humanity, who is also a land creature. This is the only day that breaks the pattern by including two acts of creation. The second spurt of creative activity on the sixth day, apart from whatever is created, gets our attention because it breaks the pattern of the other days to which we become accustomed as we read along. One might argue, just on literary grounds, that Genesis 1 emphasizes the second half of day six. Of course, because it is humanity that is created in the second half of the sixth day, Genesis 1 points to the special role for humanity in God's creation. The content of verses 26–28 indicate that humanity's special role in creation is undergirded by humanity's special relationship with God—the only creature who is created in God's image and charged to exercise dominion over the other creatures.[15] This insight about the importance of humanity also suggests at least one way the story of creation in Genesis 1 is related to the story in Genesis 2. Genesis 1 builds to the creation of humanity; Genesis 2 quickly focuses on humanity's role in God's creation. Thus, the two creation stories complement each other, even though they differ in significant ways.

Finally, we can also see that there is a pattern among the days. Days one and four, two and five, and three and six are paired (see chart on facing page[16]). The seventh day stands on its own. The order of the text is not just through the repeated pattern of each day, but by the ways the first six days are related to one another. Genesis 1 is an orderly account about the way that God brings order out of chaos. The point of the story about the goodness of God's carefully ordered creation is made not just by what the text says but by the orderly manner in which the text is arranged.

Day 1	**Day 4**
God creates night and day.	God creates the sun and moon.
Day 2	**Day 5**
God creates water and sky.	God creates the creatures of the sky and sea.
Day 3	**Day 6**
God creates the dry land (Earth).	God creates the creatures to inhabit the dry land.

By focusing on the text itself, one can hear in Genesis 1 powerful claims about God and God's world. We can affirm that this text is "true" in what it claims about God and the creation without having to take its description of the creation to be "factually accurate." After all, the point of this text is not to present a scientific theory about how the world began, an effort that would be incomprehensible in a premodern culture. Rather, Genesis 1 wants to say something about God, as is evident by the repeated references to God, who is the sole subject of the narrative's verbs, in Genesis 1. One of the most significant claims that Genesis 1 wants to make, evident by the way in which the story is told, is that the good creation depends on God. Genesis 1 describes a "world" with its words and the artistry of its composition. We as readers are then invited to enter that world—to examine the ways the world of Genesis 1 rings true to our experience, or perhaps the ways that Genesis 1 invites us to see something about God, the world, and ourselves that we had not seen until we read this story.

Notice, too, that we can read this text without needing to know who wrote it or in what circumstances. The story makes sense and its points are clear enough without knowing that this text was written by the Priestly Writers in the exile. However, if we understand that the Genesis 1 creation story was written by the Priestly Writers in the exile, this may enrich our understanding of this text. After all, for those who had experienced the exile, it seemed as if the world had collapsed into chaos and God was powerless to do anything about it. The orderly account of creation in Genesis 1 can be understood in the exile to be a story intended to counter the experience of exiles. Genesis 1 claims that the world is not chaotic, that God is not powerless, and that to be human is not an exercise in futility.

It is possible to sense the meaning of a biblical text by focusing on the text itself. However, when we know who the author of a text is and something of the circumstances in which a text was written, such understanding may enrich the meanings of a text that we have come to understand by focusing on the text itself.

So far we have used Genesis 1 to illustrate how one can understand the meanings of a biblical text by focusing on the text itself. Briefly, let us illustrate how this same approach might work with a New Testament text. In Paul's letters to the church at Corinth, 1 Corinthians 13, the so-called love chapter, is very familiar and often read at weddings. However, 1 Corinthians 13 is actually part of a longer discussion that Paul develops about "spiritual gifts." To make sense of 1 Corinthians 13, we need to start with 1 Corinthians 12, where Paul introduces the topic of spiritual gifts about which he senses there is a problem at Corinth (1 Cor. 12:1–3). Throughout 1 Corinthians 12, Paul discusses the variety but interrelated character of spiritual gifts, finally using the analogy of the interdependence of body parts (vv. 12–30). Paul's discussion in 1 Corinthians 12 then concludes with an exhortation about spiritual gifts: "But strive for the greater gifts. And I will show you a still more excellent way" (v. 31). So although Paul affirms a variety of "spiritual gifts," he thinks some are better than others, and he urges the Corinthians to strive for "the greater gifts."

This exhortation leads to 1 Corinthians 13, where Paul immediately compares two "spiritual gifts"—speaking in tongues (which Paul mentioned briefly in 1 Cor. 12:30) and love. Of these two "spiritual gifts," Paul argues in 1 Corinthians 13 why love is the greatest of the "spiritual gifts"—greater than speaking in tongues, to be sure, but also better than prophecy, or hope, or even faith! Paul's argument that love is the greatest of the spiritual gifts then leads to 1 Corinthians 14, where Paul speaks again of love, prophecy, and speaking in tongues and the ways that these were problematic for the church in Corinth.

We have given some all-too-brief attention to the logic of Paul's discussion about spiritual gifts in 1 Corinthians to show again the value of focusing on the biblical text itself. Paul was a student of ancient rhetoric—of ways of arguing or debating. This is often evident in his letters. Therefore, we need to give attention to the ways that Paul develops his arguments, attention to the text itself. Certainly to understand Paul more fully, it is important to think about the relationship of Paul's letters to the circumstances in which they were written. However, close attention to the text of Paul's letters and the careful ways in which he develops his arguments is also vital to understanding their meaning.

This interpretative approach, which focuses on the biblical text itself, is often a helpful way of engaging the Bible in churches. Because of its focus on the text, one can invite persons simply to read a biblical text as they might read any story or poem. The purpose is to enter the world of the biblical text, to be drawn into the text. Because making connections are central to learning, the connections that one encourages persons to make with this approach are between the "world of the text" and the experiences of those engaging the text. So, for instance, in reading Genesis 1, one might invite persons to reflect on some of the affirmations of the text: How do we relate to the repeated claim of Genesis 1 that God's creation is "good"? What do we make of the claim of this story that humanity occupies a central place in God's creation? What might it mean to exercise "dominion"? Regarding Paul's discussion of spiritual gifts, one might ask in a Bible study if persons ever imagined that their gifts were more important than everyone else's in their church. Or one might ask what the church would be like if everyone sought, as a first priority, to relate in "love" as Paul describes in 1 Corinthians 13.

The historical-critical interpretative approach is often frustrating to persons in the church because it requires somewhat specialized knowledge, understanding of rather technical matters that underlie biblical texts: Who wrote this? When? What was the world like then? Persons can become frustrated trying to get at this information behind the text. This approach of focusing on the text itself avoids some of those frustrations. Further, the historical-critical approach almost always raises issues of factual accuracy. Did this happen the way the biblical text describes? Of course, the issue of the Bible's factual accuracy—actually an issue about the nature, character, and purposes of the Bible—cannot and should not ultimately be avoided. Nonetheless, an interpretative approach that focuses on the text itself can allow persons with very different assumptions about the factual accuracy of the Bible to meaningfully engage biblical texts together. Some in a group may be hearing the text quite literally. Others assume a more metaphorical or less literal sense of the Bible. Yet by focusing on the text itself, this argument can at least be sidestepped for the moment to allow a mutual engagement of a biblical text. Focusing on the text itself, a group studying the Bible is invited to explore what, for instance, a text claims about God, about the church, or about what it means to be God's creatures in God's world.

A further advantage of this approach is that it can be used with children and early adolescents too young to be able to use a historical-critical approach. Children love stories—they love to hear them and in time to retell them. One of the ways that children can experience the transforming power of the Bible is as we share with them its stories. Of course, prudence is needed in choosing Bible stories appropriate for the age and experience of the child, as prudence in needed in choosing any material to be shared with children. Stories that are complicated, violent, or potentially frightening or that recount situations beyond children's life experiences or emotional maturity are well avoided. Yet when children are told age-appropriate Bible stories, they will make sense of these stories as best they can at their age. That is, they will make connections between the story and their life and experience, even if it may not be the connections that occur to adults with considerably more life experience.[17] If we take care not to impose our adult meanings on children, as children grow older and hear Bible stories repeated they will make fresh connections reflecting a richer fund of life experiences to which they can connect the biblical stories.

Again, some cautions are also in order in using an interpretative approach that focuses on the biblical text itself. First, it is also possible in this approach to concentrate on "facts" about the text—information—and lose sight of the goal of biblical study, which is transformation. When focusing on the text itself, the information that can ensnare us is different from that with a historical-critical approach. With the latter, we are tempted to get caught up in historical details that underlie and inform our understanding of the text. When focusing on the text itself, we are tempted to get caught up in the literary details of the text and forget to ask of their significance. For instance, with Genesis 1 we can become enamored with the repetition of phrases that are found in each day, or with the ways that the first six days of creation relate to one another (the pairing of days 1 and 4, and so on), but forget to ask the significance of these literary features, their implications for helping us understand the meaning of the text.

Second, we may be tempted to settle in and choose this interpretative approach that focuses on the text itself as our exclusive way of reading and interpreting the Bible. As indicated in the preceding paragraphs, this way of reading the Bible seems to avoid some of the challenging research into the historical background behind a text demanded by a historical-critical approach. Further, it can provide, at least for a while, a way around dealing with the thorny issues of factual accuracy. We need to be careful if we are tempted in this way. As we indicated in chapter 3, biblical texts were written long ago and far away in a culture much different from our own. If we focus on the biblical text itself without awareness of the historical and cultural distance of the biblical text from our own experience, we are likely to misunderstand the text. Even if we are reading a text about which we cannot be sure of the author or circumstances of composition—many psalms, for instance—we will still need to take account of the ancient Near Eastern cultural background assumed by whomever composed the psalm. Although we may focus on the text itself, there is finally no way to avoid dealing with at least some of the historical and cultural background of a biblical text. Nor, finally, is there any way that we can avoid dealing with the differences between those persons in our churches who take biblical texts literally and those who do not.

Third, in using this approach we can be tempted to think that a biblical text has a single meaning and should be understood in one way. Our experience in reading nonbiblical material should warn us of the fallacy of thinking that when we focus on the biblical text itself we will discern only one meaning. Even though everyone in a church group is reading the same biblical text, we should expect that different persons will discern very different meanings. You can speak with a colleague at work about a short editorial in the morning paper and find that you and your colleague did not understand it the same way, even though you both read the same three paragraphs.

It is certainly true that if you and several friends read the same book, you will probably each understand the meaning of the book somewhat differently, or maybe very differently. So, too, when we read the Bible, and even when we all agree that the way we will read the Bible is to focus on the text itself, different people will discern different meanings. Why is this? Because we bring to a biblical text different experiences, as we are different people, and so we make connections between the text and our experiences in different ways.

Because we who read the Bible do so out of our own experiences, we read and understand the Bible in different ways. So we must examine yet another approach to interpreting the Bible, an approach that focuses on the relationship between the Bible and its readers.

A Text Relates to Its Contemporary Readers

A text can be understood as it relates to its contemporary readers: who they are, what they value, and what they bring to their reading of the text. In figure 1, this interpretative approach is represented by line D, which connects the "Bible" box in the center of the chart to the "Reader" box in the lower right corner. This is the way that Joyce related to Genesis 1. In hearing the Genesis 1 creation story, Joyce responded initially out of her concern for environmental issues. She also responded out of her experience as a woman and her identification with women who have been oppressed or exploited because of their gender. So she is concerned about the ways that the creation stories in Genesis 1 and 2 have been read and used to justify abuse of the environment and the subordination of women to men. Joyce relates to Genesis 1 *as a contemporary reader—out of who she is, what she values, and what she brings to the text.*

This way of interpreting biblical texts understands that the meaning of any biblical text will be affected by who the reader is. If we make meaning by making connections, then persons who bring different experiences and concerns to a biblical text will perceive a text's meaning in different ways. In American culture, women have different experiences than men. Despite changes in recent decades, the care of children and such household tasks as cleaning, doing laundry, and cooking still largely fall to women. In the workplace, women doing the same work as men on average get paid less and have a difficult time in advancing beyond certain levels in most organizations. Sexual harassment of women remains an ugly social reality. Therefore, it is not surprising that many women, like Joyce, are particularly sensitive to the ways that biblical texts might be interpreted to justify exploiting or oppressing women.

Of course, it is not just women who interpret the Bible because of who they are and what they bring to their reading of the Bible. We all do this. Protestants will read the Bible differently than those who are Roman Catholic. Presbyterians will read the Bible differently than Southern Baptists or Methodists. African Americans will interpret the Bible out of their particular experiences. Those with more wealth will likely interpret the Bible differently than those who are poor. Persons from Third World countries will interpret the Bible out of their unique experiences. We could go on and on.

We must also take account of another factor when considering this interpretative approach, which focuses on the readers of the Bible. Historically, it has been white men who have been the primary public interpreters of the Bible. That is, it has been white men who have been socially and economically privileged and so in a position to earn graduate degrees in Bible studies, with which they have gotten teaching positions and the opportunity to publish their biblical interpretations. Thus, the interpretations of the Bible that are considered normative (that is, considered to be "correct") have, until very recently, been the interpretations of white men, mostly in well-paid positions in churches or institutions of higher education.

What we know, of course, is that everyone interprets by making connections between their experiences and the biblical text. The dominance of white men as the public interpreters of the Bible has meant that most of us have had little exposure to the interpretations of those with different experiences—women, racial minorities, persons economically marginalized, those from Third World countries. In this way, those of us who are part of church traditions that have mainly relied on the interpretations of white men have been exposed to rather parochial and narrow interpretations of the Bible.[18] This interpretative approach that focuses on the relationship between the text and its readers invites us to encounter a rich and challenging diversity of readings, especially those interpretations of persons who are more different than like us.[19]

Let us offer an example of this interpretative approach. In the introduction to her book on the Pentateuch (the first five books of the Old Testament), Alice Laffey describes the "feminist consciousness" that guides her reading of the Bible in this way:

> A feminist consciousness...that promotes equality, mutuality, and reciprocity between the sexes, also commits itself to peace, to empowering those human persons whom the hierarchical social organization has relegated to its lower rungs, the human persons whom society considers less powerful and who are therefore potentially more vulnerable (in First World societies, the elderly, racial minorities, gays and lesbians, the poor), and to fostering respect for and cooperation with all nonhuman participants in and inhabitants of the cosmos.[20]

Of course, many men share the concerns that Laffey describes as belonging to a "feminist consciousness," but Laffey's point is that because of the experiences of women, women are more likely to hold the perspective she describes than men.

When Laffey turns to the biblical text itself, what she calls "feminist consciousness" becomes evident in the way she interprets a text such as Genesis 1. Commenting on Genesis 1:28, God's charge that humanity exercise "dominion" over the fish, birds, and land animals, Laffey comments first:

> The verse that legitimates human domination of fish, birds, cattle, wild animals and creeping things may simply indicate that by the sixth century B.C.E. humankind used animals for farming and may have been carnivorous. Whereas certain elements of creation, once created, are self sufficient, animals are not. They are not only dependent on other elements of creation (e.g., plants need sunlight), their existence depends on the use of (and perhaps the consumption of) others. To

legitimate such domination, the author may well have found it necessary to compare humankind to God; only God could legitimately do—or legitimate what man [*sic*] needed to do—to effect human survival.[21]

We note in these comments two matters. First, Laffey stresses the interdependence of the creation, an interpretation through which we hear echoed what she has described as a "feminist consciousness" (see earlier). Yet even as we hear her feminist concerns, Laffey is aware of who the authors of this text were and when this text was written. She is using multiple interpretative approaches at once. Having reflected on what it might have meant for humans to have dominion at the time when the text was written, Laffey presses her interpretation deeper. She continues:

This interpretation does not intend to suggest that the author who produced these texts was not patriarchal; as a product of his culture, he undoubtedly was thoroughly hierarchical. What it does suggest, however, is that the ancients understood their relationship to nature very differently from how humans now understand that relationship, after three thousand years of "subduing" and "having dominion over" and legitimating that behavior with an explanation of our difference from other creatures. In fact, according to the narrative, all the animals including humans are created on the sixth day. The text has been interpreted as referring to human rationality—the ability to speak, to write, and to remember—but the text makes no mention of these qualities. Human beings continue to exaggerate the difference between themselves and other animals in spite of the fact that much is now known about the sophisticated intelligence—the memory, the ability to communicate, and so forth—of certain other animals.[22]

Although Laffey is alert to issues about the author of this text and the ancient culture that this text reflects, she also reads Genesis 1:28 out of her experience as a woman. As she indicates in the introduction to her book, she works out of a "feminist consciousness" that is committed to equality and mutuality, values she stresses when interpreting the meaning of "dominion" in Genesis 1. Although Laffey does not explicitly press the point in her reflection on Genesis 1, her interpretation has political implications. Concern for reordering social structures and policies is often characteristic of the reader-centered approach. For example, reading Genesis 1 as Laffey proposes is suggestive regarding public policy debates relating to women's issues, as well as the environment.

Again, the approach under discussion understands biblical texts as they relate to contemporary readers—who they are, what they value, and what they bring to their reading of the text. Materials reflecting it are readily available, and more and more become available all the time. It is an approach to interpreting the Bible from which we can learn much.

At one level this approach reminds all of us who read and interpret the Bible that we inevitably do so out of our experiences and assumptions. Our experiences and assumptions are shaped in many ways: by the churches that have nurtured us, by our social and economic status, by our gender and race, by our educational background, by the fact that we are Western and American (or whatever broad cultural and national groups have exerted influence on us), and so on. All these factors are like lenses that filter how we read and understand the Bible.

Yet we are often unaware of the deep cultural influences that shape our readings of biblical texts. An interpretative approach that stresses the relationship between the text and its reader invites us— all of us—to become self-consciously aware of the ways our experiences and backgrounds shape the ways we read and interpret the Bible. Thus, as we are teaching the Bible, it is important to ask ourselves and those whom we are teaching to reflect on why we read and interpret biblical texts as we do. In doing so, we are asking that we and those we teach become aware of the many cultural influences, the personal experiences, the religious and ecclesial experiences that shape how we read and interpret biblical texts.

At another level, this approach is an invitation to expand our interpretations of biblical texts. By using resources that reflect the interpretations of persons who live in different circumstances from our own or who have had very different experiences from our own, we are encouraged to hear biblical texts in new ways, ways that we ourselves could never imagine. In a dialogue in a racially mixed Old Testament class about the exodus, the younger white students encountered the powerful witness of several African American students about the oppression they had experienced in "white America." Although initially defensive, the white students slowly heard the pain of their African American colleagues. The discussion began to explore the danger of the white students' too easy identification with oppressed slaves and the insight that many of us who are part of the majority culture in America may need to identify with the pharaoh's role in the exodus story. It is challenging to hear biblical stories interpreted by women, by persons who are racial minorities, by persons who live in Third World countries. To invite intentionally these "other" voices to our Bible studies—by the resources we use or, if possible, by persons' actual presence in the group—broadens our understanding of biblical texts and helps us see beyond the interpretations that our own experiences may allow us.

There are some potential problems with the use of this interpretative approach. Sometimes the biblical interpretations of persons with very different experiences or who live in very different places may seem quite "strange" to us and to those we are teaching.[23] A temptation will be to judge these "other" interpretations as wrong, or worse. If we choose to engage the biblical interpretations of those who are not like us, then it is important to stand open to their experiences and interpretations. These encounters add another dimension to the intercultural process of biblical study. These "others," are also children of God who with us struggle to understand who God is, what God is about, and how we humans are to respond to God—though from contexts and perspectives often quite different from those to which we are accustomed. We gain nothing if, encountering the interpretation of these persons, we dismiss them or the ways they understand the Bible. But if we are willing to stand open to those who view the world with different eyes from ours, then we may be moved to new insights about who God is, what God is about, and how we humans are to respond to God.

There is another potential problem with this reader-focused interpretative approach. We believe that if the readings shared in the study of a biblical text are undertaken by readers who are very much like one another (and many congregations are quite similar in terms of race, economic status, theological orientation, and so on), little will be gained. A group of readers of the same gender or from the same racial, economic, or cultural group will likely read and interpret a text out of very similar experiences and will only reinforce one another's understandings of biblical texts. When persons who bring significantly different life experiences are not present (either in person or through the resources being used), there will be little possibility for people to understand a biblical text from a fresh or challenging perspective. This interpretative approach that focuses on the readers is certainly useful in diverse groups where those present are likely to bring different perspectives to their reading of the Bible. If the study group is largely homogenous, then this reader-centered interpretative approach requires that the leader of the Bible study introduce students to the voices of persons not represented in the group itself by identifying resources that will expand the group's consideration of texts.

Summary and Implications for Teaching the Bible

In this chapter we have discussed four interpretative approaches to reading the Bible: (1) an approach that takes the text literally; (2) an approach that focuses on the author of a biblical text and the circumstances of its composition; (3) an approach that focuses on the literary features of a biblical text; and (4) an approach that focuses on the perspectives brought to a text by its readers. Some important principles regarding the interpretation of the Bible have grow out of this discussion. We believe it is vital that teachers of the Bible in the church keep these principles in mind as they shape their own teaching.

1. *Be aware of and intentional about the interpretative approaches we use in teaching.* How one reads and interprets a biblical text is critical to what one teaches. Teachers have an ethical responsibility to be intentional interpreters of the Bible. It is also important that teachers be aware of the interpretative approach of any resources they use in order to engage these with integrity in their teaching.

2. *Be aware of the interpretative approaches used by those whom we teach.* Often those who study scriptures in churches are not aware of the assumptions with which they read the Bible or the dominant

interpretative approach they use to understand the text. Only teachers who develop an awareness of the interpretative approaches being used by their students will be in a position to make sense of their students' responses to biblical texts, to understand the different interpretations being offered, and to challenge students to look at biblical texts in fresh ways.

3. *Be respectful of the different interpretative approaches our students use.* We have expressed our own reservations about the literalistic interpretative approach and indicated that, even though many persons in churches do interpret the Bible in this way, we cannot commend it. However, those of us who do not read the Bible in a literal way need to recognize there are those who do, and we need to respect them and have in mind strategies by which they can be included in the study of scripture in the church.

4. *The use of multiple interpretative approaches is vital.* It is important to remember that the different approaches described here view biblical texts in very different ways and therefore ask different questions about the text. In our judgment, the richest Bible studies occur when teachers of the Bible are willing to use multiple interpretative approaches. Each of the different interpretative approaches we have discussed can contribute to a deeper understanding of a text. Only by examining a text from a variety of perspectives are we likely to see the rich ways the Bible may address us.

5. *Give careful thought and attention to the interpretive approach used initially.* While we finally urge the use of a variety of interpretative approaches, it is inevitable that we need to begin with one approach or another. Care should be taken with regard to which approach to choose. The choice of an initial approach may be influenced by a variety of factors, including the interpretative disposition of those engaged in the study, judgment about how to respect the interpretative disposition of those engaged in the study even while challenging them, the age of participants, the homogeneity or diversity of the group, the openness of the group to new ideas or perspectives, the skill of the teacher in using one or another interpretive approach, and the kinds of resources for studying the Bible available to both students and the teachers

6. *Remember that the ultimate goal of teaching the Bible is transformation.* We believe that no matter which interpretative

approaches are used, it is vital to remember that the final goal of our teaching is transformation. Although information is indispensable for serious engagement of the Bible, our goal as teachers is not to help students just acquire more information. Rather, our ultimate goal of teaching the Bible is transformation—the transformation of persons to be faithful servants of Jesus Christ and the coming reign of God.

5

Teaching the Bible: Putting It All Together

We must be preaching and teaching the Bible in the church. It is a claim with which we began this book and a claim that continues to ground us. Yet we know that this claim is not enough for those of us called to preach and teach. We also need to consider *how* we do this. It has been the aim of this book to explore this important question of "how," and in our doing so we have named some important principles we believe need to shape and guide our work as teachers.

Being mindful that our brains need repetition for memory to form, let us rehearse these principles once again. In order to be sensitive to how the brain works and how our students learn, as teachers we need to remember the following:

- Teach to and for connection.

- Emotions are critical to learning.

- Teach to challenge, not to threaten.

- All learning begins with sensory experiences.

- Teach to a variety of learning styles and intelligences.

- The key words are *rehearse, reflect,* and *connect.*

Knowing how to teach is more than acquiring a set of skills and techniques. The knowledges we need invite us to remember the following:

- Know thyself.

- *How* we teach depends on *who* we are teaching.

- *How* we teach depends on *where* we teach.

- Know your content.

- How we teach is shaped by the images of teacher we hold and by the approach to teaching we use.

- Knowing *how* to choose and *when* to use a method, tool, or technique is key.

Teaching the Bible is an experience in intercultural education. Important principles to guide our efforts at such education include the following:

- Remember that we are all cultural beings.

- Teach for cultural awareness.

- Teach for cultural appreciation and respect.

- Teach for intercultural competence.

And finally, teaching the Bible calls for an awareness of the range of assumptions we bring to the interpretation of texts. Principles to guide our work with the issues of interpretation we encounter as teachers include the following:

- Be aware of and intentional about the interpretative approaches we use in teaching.

- Be aware of the interpretative approaches used by those whom we teach.

- Be respectful of the different interpretative approaches our students use.

- The use of multiple interpretative approaches is vital.

- Give careful thought and attention to the interpretive approach used initially.

We hope that these principles will be useful in shaping and forming our teaching of the Bible in helpful ways, and that they also will assist us in assessing and evaluating the curriculum resources we choose to use with our students.

But a list of principles does not seem adequate for our aim of helping us become better teachers of the Bible in the church. How one puts these principles into practice is also vital knowledge for our work. In this final chapter we want to explore just that—how to put these into practice. Whether designing a study from the beginning or using prepared curriculum resources, the principles we have named are important tools for helping us do our work as teachers.

The question we asked ourselves was how we could best help you, our reader, explore putting these into practice. One of the approaches we thought about was providing some sample Bible studies that illustrate the principles. But good Bible studies are always unique and particular to a given setting or situation, even when a teacher is using already prepared curriculum resources. There are still lots of decisions one has to make, even with prepared curriculum.

Instead of sample Bible studies, we decided it would be most helpful to take a look at the kind of process a teacher might engage when using these principles to prepare to teach the Bible in his or her context. To do this, we invite you now into one pastor's study for a look at how she uses the principles as she prepares to teach the Bible.

In the Teacher's Workshop

Let's return to Pastor Mary, whom we first met in chapter 4, preparing to teach a newly formed women's evening Bible study. As she is preparing for this study, the pastor is also thinking about some other teaching responsibilities coming up soon on her calendar. Her confirmation class, young people mostly in the ninth grade, is ready to begin an important unit of study in which they will undertake an overview of the Bible. Also, Pastor Mary does a weekly children's time in worship, and the congregation's worship council has asked her to focus these more on Bible stories than she has been. She has cleared several hours for preparation from her schedule, and when she closes her study door, the room becomes a teacher's workshop.

As Pastor Mary considers the first night's gathering of the women's Bible study, there are several areas that invite her attention. First, she knows that one of the important teacher knowledges is who her students are. She thinks about who will likely attend. She thumbs through the church directory and also looks at the notes from two women who have been organizing the group. She anticipates a group of about fifteen women, ranging in age from their mid-thirties to their late fifties. The majority of the women are married, and many have children ranging in ages from elementary school through college. They come with different learning styles and different issues at the forefront of their lives. Mary continues to reflect on what she knows about these women and also realizes she needs to give the same kind of thought to both her confirmation class and the children who gather for the weekly children's time in worship. She wants to take seriously who her students are, knowing that *who* we teach shapes *how* we teach.

Mary knows that most of the women are employed outside the home and have been unable to attend daytime opportunities of scripture study that the congregation has offered for many years. Thus, they have not regularly engaged in Bible study. She anticipates that many of them will likely take the Bible rather literally, in large part because they simply have not thought of it in any other way. At the same time, the women who helped organize this study have spoken with her several times in recent months about how to understand this or that biblical passage and have even borrowed books from her. Mary knows she needs to be sensitive to the different interpretive approaches that may be present in the group.

Pastor Mary knows she cannot ignore the cultural context within which she teaches. In the upper middle-class suburb where the congregation is located, the church members are for the most part well educated, and many persons hold professional positions. Culturally, her congregation to a large measure shares the general values of Western and American cultures. However, some persons only have high school educations and are financially more marginal. From conversations with them, Mary knows that some of these people are more dubious about the "American dream," and some are even bitter because they feel on the margins in their upwardly mobile suburban community.

Although the denomination of which Pastor Mary's congregation is a part is recognized nationally for its "liberal" social and theological positions, Mary knows that many in her congregation have strong disagreements about the denomination's stances. One woman who is coming to the Bible study has visited a nearby church that describes itself as "Bible-believing" and has thought about joining that church. In terms of their approach to the Bible, Mary thinks that the largest plurality of her congregation is pietistic, but she knows there is a significant group who would be more moralistic and a vocal minority who are doctrinal. In terms of its ecclesial culture, the congregation is rather diverse, and Mary knows this diversity will be a challenge in her new Bible study group.

Because many of the women are new to Bible study, Pastor Mary has been thinking for some days about what part of the Bible with which to begin. She knows that some of the women read the psalms devotionally. Mary, however, knows herself well, and she does not enjoy teaching the psalms all that much. She more enjoys teaching narrative portions of the Bible. Applying the principle "Know thyself," she wants to begin with something about which she can be genuinely enthused, trusting that her enthusiasm will invite her students' enthusiasm.

She thought about Matthew's gospel, because it is presently the gospel assigned by the lectionary. But the assigned Sunday lectionary readings are already halfway through Matthew's gospel, and she believes it would be awkward, if not confusing, to begin a Bible study at the beginning of Matthew on Tuesday evening while the Sunday reading is from Matthew 18.

Finally, Mary decides on Genesis. The women, even those without much biblical background, will be somewhat familiar with some parts of Genesis, such as the creation and flood stories. They will already have some connections with which to work. And Genesis should be comfortable enough that even those without much biblical background won't feel intimidated. It is the kind of narrative text she likes and, furthermore, it's a new Bible study group, so they might as well start at the beginning. As she thinks some more about Genesis, she also likes the possibility that she can connect her preparation for the women's Bible study to her confirmation teaching and maybe even a Sunday morning children's time or two as well.

With her decision to teach Genesis, Mary begins her preparation by doing some interpretative work with Genesis 1, the text on which she will focus the first night. While she has worked with this text many times, she spends a good deal of time both doing her own interpretative work with the text and reading from several commentaries. She knows that to teach effectively, she needs to know the content of the lesson thoroughly. In addition to detailed notes about specific issues in the text, she also makes some notes to summarize key interpretative insights that she wants to work with in shaping her teaching plan:

1. She makes notes about what she and commentators have seen about the literary or artistic design of Genesis 1, the many repetitions in the text and the way the text builds to a climax on day six. Focusing on the literary structure might be a way to engage the text in a non-threatening way.

2. Her reading in commentaries reminds her again about the importance of understanding the historical setting in which this text was written, the Babylonian exile. She notes where she has more detailed information about Judah's exile of 587 B.C.E. In the margin she notes, "Important, but go slow." She wants to introduce this way of reading Genesis 1, but is aware that some will find this approach threatening. She wants to teach to challenge, not threaten.

3. The commentaries also help her identify the ways in which Genesis 1 reflects very different cultural assumptions from those of persons reading the text in the twenty-first century. One commentary stressed that contemporary people will bring scientific questions to this text, concerned with the origins of the world, whereas such a concern would have been unknown to persons when the text was written. Glancing back at one commentary, Mary sees that she has written "yes" in the margin where the commentator noted this cultural difference. She knows she will need to help her students develop some awareness of these cultural differences.

4. One commentary in particular reminds Mary that modern people will hear the language of Genesis 1, "dominion," as heavily patriarchal. Although the world of ancient Israel was patriarchal, "dominion" in Genesis 1 might imply more

caretaking (cf. Psalm 72) than domination. She knows that for one of the new group's organizers, this will be a very important issue, so she better be prepared to address this concern. Teaching for cultural awareness, affirmation, and respect with regard to ancient Israel will need her attention.

Pastor Mary is satisfied that her study of Genesis 1 has given her the perspective of several interpretative approaches.

However, Mary knows that it is important to be intentional about one's initial interpretative approach when teaching the Bible. She again thinks of the diversity of perspectives the women will bring, and she particularly remembers some of the women who are likely to read Genesis 1 more literally. In time she would like to do something with a historical-critical approach so the women can see the creation story related to the historical context in which it arose. But she concludes that this will be too threatening for some of the participants at the first meeting of the new group. Therefore, she opts to use a more literary approach as her starting point. Thinking ahead, she imagines that she will take a similar literary approach to Genesis 2—3 in the second class session. Then during the third session, she thinks, she may be able to ask persons to compare the two accounts of creation. When the group is in a position to raise questions about the differences between the two creation stories, Mary believes she can introduce a historical-critical interpretation that will not be so threatening to them.

With the careful interpretive work done and a decision about her initial interpretative approach made, Mary next turns to the design of her lesson. How should she approach teaching Genesis 1 the first night the evening Bible study meets? She also remembers her confirmation class and the children's time. How might she approach this text with youth and children? But first things first, so she begins by focusing on the lesson design for the women's Bible study group.

As is usual for Mary, she pulls a legal-size pad from her desk and begins her lesson plan by simply sketching some ideas. Later she will tidy up her plan, but for now she just wants to give her own brain some imagining room. She jots down some notes to herself at the top of the page:

- "Remember who will be there! And remember they are not all the same."

- "What am I going to do to engage these women—particularly those in the group who are less verbal or perhaps a little intimidated because they are new to Bible study?"

- "Challenge, but don't threaten them. Get them interested so they'll come back."

- "The Bible comes from a different cultural world—we have to keep working to understand this!"

- "Help them make some connections—but how? Think about this!"

- "How will they be better disciples—how will we be a better church when this session is over?"

Pastor Mary focuses on her last question first. She wants to do more than share information about Genesis 1. She is aware that when she knows a lot about a text, she is very likely to get so wrapped up in sharing information she neglects the central purpose of Bible study, which she understands to be transformation. So as she thinks about her first session, she wants to be sure that participants are invited to ponder some kind of transformation.

Having done her interpretative work, she decides that she wants to focus on the meaning of being created in God's image—a claim that in its cultural context Mary understands to be about God's expectation that humanity will be caretakers of God's creation. Pastor Mary, in reflecting about the women she will be teaching, thinks that this focus will offer participants the possibility of challenge, a fresh way to look at the text, and an opportunity to make connections with their life experience. However, aware that persons will hear the text out of their own experience, Mary notes some other themes she will underscore as she has an opportunity. Noting these themes will help her remember them and affirm them in the give and take of the class:

- The world is carefully and graciously ordered by God.

- God, who orders chaos, makes life possible.

- The world God has made is good.

- The whole of God's created order is connected and interdependent.

As Mary prepares, she is not sure which, if any, of these affirmations from Genesis 1 (or others she cannot even think of) class members might identify.

As Mary is thinking about the focus of her lesson, she finds that her mind is wandering. She recalls an incident in seminary when she offered an idea in class that was rather curtly cut off by the professor, who clearly wanted to go in another direction with the discussion. Mary recalled the frustration of that painful experience and her resolve not to teach like that. This recollection reminds Mary of the image of a teacher she holds. She sees herself as the guide for the class, but she knows she cannot determine how students will make connections. Of course, she needs to be clear about her content, Genesis 1, so if need be she can clarify matters related to the literary, cultural, or historical features of the text and the implications of these for the text's theological claims. But she also wants to remain flexible and responsive to the connections her students are able to make. Mary wants to move the class to focus on the meaning of humanity created in the image of God because she thinks this claim offers rich possibilities for the women to make connections with their lives. But she knows that those in the class, out of their own experiences, may be drawn to other parts of the text, and these might become the focus of the class, around which students will make the most important connections.

With this preliminary thinking about the focus in mind, Mary now begins to think more concretely about the lesson design. She often uses Groome's shared praxis approach because she, with Groome, believes that education happens best when students and teachers are fully engaged together in the educational process. Mary is comfortable with Groome's approach for several reasons: (1) It stresses beginning where folks are as they name their current praxis; (2) it encourages dialogue, an effective way for adults to be active participants in learning; and (3) it moves participants toward making decisions about the implications and significance of what they have been studying—in other words, it aims at transformation. So Mary begins to plot out her lesson step-by-step. She is relieved that the sessions will be ninety minutes, so she has plenty of time to develop her lesson. She makes a mental note that she has only one hour with her confirmation class and just minutes with the children. She will need to take another approach, but it is just as well. Neither the youth nor the children will have the attention to engage one biblical text for more than an hour. Even with adults, she will need to keep the class moving or they will not stay engaged.

What would it mean with Genesis 1, she asks, for participants to "name their current praxis"? In a minute it is clear to her. She needs to invite the women to share how they already understand this well-known text. Now ideas for the class start to come quickly for Mary, and an outline of the class, following Groome's shared praxis approach, begins to emerge:

Focusing Activity. Pastor Mary, after welcome, a prayer, and introductions, will read Genesis 1 aloud and then allow some moments of silence for participants to reflect on the text. Knowing she needs to engage a variety of senses in the learning process, she will have Bibles available so everyone can see, as well as hear, the text.

Naming/Expressing Current Praxis. Mary will then invite participants to share their responses to the familiar text that they have just heard—be it the emotions the text evokes, the message they hear, or a time when they remember the text being used that has stuck with them. Mary also has a tape of James Weldon Johnson's rendition of Genesis 1 from "God's Trombones, The Creation."[1] After the initial discussion, she will play the tape and seek further responses this setting of the text evokes. Mary has found that people often find this rendition emotionally powerful, and the tape provides an alternative sensory experience.

Critical Reflection on Praxis. Mary hopes that the initial discussions of Genesis 1 will have engaged participants with the text. Next, she wants to move directly toward her intended focus, the meaning of humanity created in the image of God. She shapes a question that she hopes will move the group toward this focus. Actually, she decides to ask the same basic question in two ways, knowing that different persons might hear her one way and not the other: (1) How does Genesis 1 understand what it means to be human? and (2) How does Genesis 1 see the role of humankind in

God's creation? Mary will allow the women to discuss these questions for a few minutes while she briefly notes the gist of their responses on the white board in the room. She hopes (but is not certain) that the group might explicitly identify the phrase "in the image of God" as a way Genesis 1 talks about humanity's role in the creation.

Mary's intent is to zero in on this key phrase of her focus after a few minutes. If it has already been identified, she will call the group's attention to it on the white board; if it has not been identified, she will state the phrase as her contribution to the discussion. With the phrase now before them, Mary will ask the women what this phrase suggests to them. She imagines that she will clear some space on the white board around the "image of God" phrase and summarize in short statements the responses offered. As she thinks about what may happen, she knows she must be prepared if the group is totally confused by the phrase "in the image of God" and cannot respond. If that is the case, she will move quickly to the next step in her lesson plan. On the other hand, the group (or someone in the group) might also be able to articulate rather well what this phrase is about. If that is the case, Mary will affirm the articulation and skip or shorten some of what she next intends.

Making Accessible the Christian Story or Vision. After the women have had a few minutes to reflect on the meaning of humanity's being created in the image of God, it will be time to both deepen and broaden the sense of this phrase in the context of Genesis 1, and Mary has several ideas for doing so. She knows that exactly how she proceeds at this point in the class session will depend on what happens in the prior discussion. On the one hand, she wants to clarify and deepen whatever understandings of "the image of God" have emerged from the prior conversation. On the other hand, she wants to broaden the women's understanding of this by showing how in Genesis 1 this vision of the role of humanity in creation relates to the broader unfolding of the chapter. She is clear that for this portion of the session, she will engage more in didactic instruction even as she will leave space for give-and-take. She outlines the sequence of issues that she wants to present as follows:

First, Mary will attempt to make the story of creation accessible by deepening the participants' understanding of the phrase "the image of God." She makes careful notes so she can explain how "image of God" might have been heard in an ancient culture. In ancient times the emissary of a king was one who literally bore the king's image through official documents to indicate he was authorized to represent the king in some matter. In Genesis 1, for humanity to bear God's image is to see humanity as God's emissary, God's authorized agent or representative to God's creation. Mary underscores these words in her notes: "While this way of viewing 'image of God' may seem strange to us, it can be a powerful image from which we can learn. This text claims that God intends us to be caretakers of God's creation." Mary knows that there will be a tendency by some in the class to view the ancient culture out of which the creation story comes as primitive and antiquarian. She hopes to encourage cultural appreciation and respect by emphasizing how creative and challenging the idea that humanity is created in God's image is.

Second, Mary wants to broaden her students' understanding of the claim that humanity is created in God's image by showing how this claim fits into the chapter as it unfolds. Here, she will attempt to make accessible the creation story in Genesis 1 by calling attention to its literary details or artistic features to support her affirmation that the idea of humanity created in the image of God is central to Genesis 1.

She quickly realizes that her students will need to "see" the features of Genesis 1 that she wants to hold before them, so her teaching at this point will need to emphasize visual learning. Mary begins to design some overhead transparencies. (She makes a note to talk to the administrative board about the purchase of equipment to allow the use of PowerPoint technology. *Wouldn't that be a neat way to do this?* she thinks.) One transparency illustrates the repeated pattern of each day of creation. Another shows the pattern of the seven days and how they are paired (one and four, two and five, and so on). A third focuses on the climactic sixth day of creation to show details of this section of the text. With this last transparency she will be able to reinforce the significance of the claim that humanity is created in the image of God, but now understood in the broader context of Genesis 1.

Although Mary envisions that she will do much of the talking during this portion of her lesson, she writes on her sheet at the end, "Questions????" She knows that even while talking and using transparencies, she needs to be alert to keep the women engaged and to remind them that their questions and comments are welcome at any point.

Integrating the Christian Story with the Students' Own Stories or Visions. Mary remembers the importance of rehearsing, reflecting, and connecting when teaching for learning. Having now *rehearsed* the creation story in Genesis 1 and having highlighted a particular focus for her class, she decides that this is the point in the lesson to allow intentional time to *reflect.* Aware of her own tendency to speak too much while teaching and that she will have been speaking a lot, she decides that the group will reflect best if she is able to pose some well-thought questions. She also decides that she will ask the women to form smaller groups of three or four to discuss the questions initially. This gives the quieter women in the group a chance to talk and be heard. It can enhance this reflective time for everyone. She will move back into the total group after a few minutes.

Although she knows that she cannot predict with certainty how the class will unfold, she imagines that the following series of questions might encourage reflection particularly on what she hopes will emerge as a central focus of this lesson, the claim that humanity is created in God's image:

- Do you agree that Genesis 1 builds to day six? If so, what significance do you see in that?

- How do you hear the claim of Genesis 1 that humanity is created in God's image?

After some time for reflection on these questions both in small groups and in the class as a whole, Mary knows she needs to draw this session to a conclusion. She is ready to encourage the women to make connections between Genesis 1 and their lives.

Deciding and Responding for Lived Christian Faith. Because Mary intends to return to the material in Genesis 1 from a historical-critical perspective in two weeks, she does not feel pressed to explore exhaustively the connections between Genesis 1 and the lives of the women at this first session. At the same time, she is clear that her goal in teaching the Bible is transformation. Further, she knows that, educationally, unless there is a connection, there is no learning. So she wonders, How can I encourage the group to make connections but keep it simple?

She again decides to have the women move into small discussion groups and ask them to discuss two interrelated questions, with directions to the groups to be sure that everyone who wants to speak be given an opportunity. The questions she decides to pose are these:

- What would it mean for you to live "in the image of God"?

- What would it mean for us as a church to live "in the image of God"?

After some minutes of group discussion, Mary will ask the groups to share as they are comfortable and as time permits. She will then conclude the session with a brief prayer and remind the group to read Genesis 2—3 for the second session.

Mary's time in her teacher's workshop is about over. The confirmation class and children's time will have to wait until tomorrow, but she has accomplished a lot. In the few minutes she has remaining to work, she remembers that she has not thought about the setup of the room. She will use one of the church meeting rooms that has a large table and comfortable chairs. It will have ample space for fifteen to eighteen people. She will ask the church janitor to carry Bibles to the room in case some persons forget theirs. There is a white board and a drop-down screen at one end of the room, and she will need both; there is already a tape player in the room.

This room will do nicely, but Mary knows that the space can enhance her teaching. How might she use the space itself to invite reflection on Genesis 1? There is a bulletin board, and she thinks about what to place on it. The first thing she remembers is a picture she has at home, a photo from NASA that is a full-color picture of the world taken from space. She will bring that picture on the first night. However, because she wants to focus on the meaning of humanity in the image of God, she walks down the hall to the church school resource room, where there is a picture file. There, she locates a large folder of pictures of people from around the world. These pictures, she thinks, will be perfect. She selects a dozen or so to hang around the NASA picture of the world. She is confident that even without commenting on these pictures, they will set a tone for the lesson she intends. The pictures enrich the sensory experience of the participants, have a certain emotional impact, and will help engage persons whose learning style is more visual. Mary has worked hard and has a lesson plan in mind for the first meeting of the women's evening Bible study and some thoughts for future sessions.

The next day she types a summary lesson plan (see this at the end of the chapter) but also has some time to think about her other teaching responsibilities with the confirmation class and during the children's time in worship. As she thinks about these assignments, she knows she will not be able to do with either the adolescents or the children that which she attempted with the women of her evening Bible study. With these other teaching responsibilities, she will need to take account of the biological and cognitive development of her students; their life experience, with which she will need to connect if learning is to take place; and the setting in which she will be undertaking the teaching of these youth and children.

As she thinks about the youth, two students come to Pastor Mary's mind. Angie is fourteen, almost fifteen. She is physically mature for her age, but Mary has also experienced her to be emotionally and cognitively mature as well. In discussions of some complex issues, Angie exhibits self-awareness and emotional control beyond her years, and it is also clear she has the ability to form clear ideas and articulate them even about abstract concepts. Angie could talk about the church as a community of God's people who serve God in the world. In Piaget's categories, Angie was mostly a formal operations thinker. (See chapter 2.) Pastor Mary sees that Angie is poised on the doorstep of adulthood and that in many ways she could probably participate in the women's evening Bible study.

Then there is Sam, just fourteen though he looks even younger. His more limited physical development is further mirrored in his emotional and cognitive abilities. Sometimes the other young people tease Sam about his lack of maturity. Pastor Mary knows it is important to set a safe climate for her students and wants to be alert to prevent such teasing.

Pastor Mary has observed that Sam has a difficult time sitting still and that his somewhat volatile emotions are transparent on his face and in his posture. Although Sam is good at recalling factual information, when a conversation becomes abstract, he struggles and is quickly bored. In Piaget's terms, Sam is still very much concrete operational in his thinking. When the class was discussing the church, he was one of the first to respond by indicating that when he thought of the church, he thought of the church building.

As Pastor Mary ran through the list of the other young people in her confirmation class, she could almost locate each one somewhere between Angie and Sam in terms of physical, emotional, and cognitive development. She knows that a major challenge she faces in teaching the confirmation class is the diverse stages of development of the young people. Their developmental diversity compounds the complexity of teaching this group because the youth also mirror the diversity of their parents and their cultural contexts in many other respects. Mary wonders how she can engage these young people in a way that will help them make connections with their life experience. How can Bible study with her confirmation class also be transformational?

Mary decides that what she will need to do is offer the confirmation class students who are more emotionally or cognitively developed an opportunity to engage Genesis 1 as they are able. At the same time, Mary recognizes that she must keep the class activities diverse and interesting enough so that those young people less emotionally and cognitively developed can stay engaged. Her experience tells her that they will make some connections as they are able and that if she can make the experience interesting enough, they will re-engage the material later when they might be able to make connections reflecting greater maturity and life experience.

Mary decides that some of what she intends with the women's group she will retain with the youth. Her initial interpretative approach will be literary. She still wants to emphasize what it means to be human in God's creation and, though she knows it will be difficult for some (because the idea is too abstract for them), she starts to focus on the phrase "in the image of God." Finally, she decides to use Groome as her basic approach to teaching. What can she do in one hour?

Pastor Mary gets out her notepad and begins to sketch ideas:
Focusing Activity. Mary thinks it would be too tedious if she

were to read aloud Genesis 1, and because not all the young people read well, she decides not to have them read it quietly by themselves either. Mary pulls the text of Genesis 1 up on her computer and begins to experiment. She soon sees a way to divide the chapter among several readers. She will print out the parts and be sure that sections of the text with more difficult words are given to the better readers. Still, she thinks she can divide the text so that everyone will have at least some part to read.

Naming and Expressing Current Praxis. Although Mary used "God's Trombones" with the women's Bible study, she thinks that the young people will not respond well to this presentation of the text. She cannot think of an alternative. She would like the students to make a collage of what they hear in Genesis 1, but she knows this activity in itself would take a lot of time, and even more time to share and discuss it. She will attempt to include some hands-on activity later in the lesson.

With just an hour for the class, she decides to keep this part of her lesson plan simple. Mary will have a copy of Genesis 1 for everyone in the class. Working as a total group, the class first will summarize the story day by day. Mary will use the large white board in the class to draw a crude image to symbolize each day. They will laugh at her art, but that's in part what she wants. It will keep the class engaged. When they have quickly reviewed the seven days of creation, she will then indicate that she thinks Genesis 1 should be read as a story like many other stories. So, she will ask, if Genesis 1 is read as a story, what is the most important part of the story and why? Mary is confident that for most of the students this will not be very difficult, and she thinks she can help others see that the story's climax comes on day six. She will summarize this discussion by underscoring the importance of God's creation of humanity in Genesis 1.

Making Accessible the Christian Story. Mary will begin this part of her lesson by indicating that she wants to think with the class about what this story understands regarding the role of humans in God's creation. She will call attention to the phrase "God created humankind in his image" (v. 27) and then ask the young people to turn their chairs so they can talk to two or three people near them. She will ask them to talk with one another about the word *image.*What is an "image," and what are some examples of "images" they can identify? She will give them a few minutes and then invite the sharing of their responses.

Anticipating their responses (or to supplement them), Mary makes a list of some "images" she will bring to class: a mirror, a photograph of herself, a coin and paper bill with an image of a figure from American history on it, the portrait of the previous pastor who retired but is remembered by most of those in the class. Mary will draw from these as the groups share their understanding of the meaning of "image." She will summarize by trying to draw together what we today understand when we think of an "image."

After sharing ideas about the meaning of "image," Pastor Mary will use the same basic material she used with the women to explain how people long ago used to think about "image." To be created in the image of God is a way the story in Genesis 1 indicates that humans are to be God's ambassadors or representatives. Mary's central point will be about the role of humans in God's creation. However, by focusing on the meaning of "image" in the ancient world of the Bible, Pastor Mary hopes that some of the more cognitively mature students will also begin to see that the Bible comes from a different "world" than our own, a lesson that will serve them well as they continue to study the Bible.

Integrating the Christian Story. Mary has often asked people to bring their old picture magazines to church for use in educational classes. She intends to have a pile of magazines and some scissors available. She will ask that everyone find two pictures that for them show people acting "in the image of God." She will not give them very long to find these, or some will start to become bored and act out. She will then ask everyone to share one picture. When everyone has shared, she will have a large poster board headed "In the Image of God," to which the students will glue their pictures.

Deciding and Responding. Pastor Mary wants to encourage the confirmation class to think not only of themselves as individuals but also about the church as a whole. As long as she has been the pastor of this church, the confirmation class has been involved in some service project. She decides that this year she will use this lesson to have the students begin thinking about this service project. So as the final activity of the class, Mary will ask the class this question: "What kinds of things might we as a class do together so we would be acting 'in the image of God'?" She will place the ideas that surface on the white board.

At the conclusion of the class, Pastor Mary decides that she will (a) emphasize in one or two sentences that humans are created in God's image to be caretakers of God's world; (b) indicate that at next week's class, the class as a whole will decide how they will do something together to experience what it is to act "in God's image"; and (c) offer a closing prayer asking that everyone remember in the next week that they are created in God's image to care for God's world.

Turning her attention now to her time with the children in worship, she knows she will have only a few minutes with them, and they are quite young. Most of the children who come forward for children's time are four to seven years old. In Piaget's terms, these children are preoperational and so have difficulty distinguishing truth, fantasy, and realism. Their language skills, although developing, are still limited, as is their sense of space and time. Pastor Mary knows that the best approach is to share a biblical story without attempting to tell children what the story means. They will make their own connections and, if the meaning is left open, will be able to revisit the story later and make new connections. Pastor Mary knows that whatever she has done with the women's Bible study or confirmation class will not be of much help when she is teaching the children. She will need to take a very different approach.

Mary reads through Genesis 1, trying to imagine what to do. As she reads, it becomes clear to her that even reading this story from the Bible will not be appropriate because the language is far beyond that which four- to seven-year-olds can understand. Yet Pastor Mary wants to affirm for the children of her congregation that God has provided for us a good home in the wonderful creation in which we live. How can she communicate this?

Because Mary only has a few minutes during the worship service, she decides that she will attempt something quite limited while she is with the children and then enlist the cooperation of the children's church school teachers to enrich what she will be attempting during worship. For the worship time, Mary begins to imagine a conversation with the children that will lead to a little litany, a litany that will be a summary of Genesis 1. She makes some notes about how this time may unfold.

She will first show the children her NASA picture of the world and talk about how beautiful our world is; she will supplement this with some pictures of nature (trees, plants, animals, and so on) and, finally, some pictures of different people—all to show and say to the children, we live in a beautiful world. As she is talking, Mary will also affirm to the children that the Bible, the church's special book, tells us that God has given us the beautiful world.

She decides to ask the children to join her in a brief prayer to thank God for our world, and the line the children are to say is, "Thank you, God." Mary then composes a litany based on Genesis 1 that she will also include in the bulletin so the whole congregation can pray with the children. She thinks of some simple physical gestures she can teach the children to involve them kinesthetically in the litany. She decides to have them bring their hands together in a posture of prayer as they say the words "Thank you," and to lift their hands and arms upward and out as though reaching toward God when they say the word "God." She will invite the whole congregation to join in these gestures too. Here is the litany she composes:

God, you give us daytime and nighttime.
Thank you, God.
God, you give us sky and air.
Thank you, God.
God, you give us land, rivers, lakes, and oceans.
Thank you, God.
God, you give us the moon and stars to light the night, and the sun to light the day.
Thank you, God.
God, you give us flowers and trees, plants that give us food, and plants that are wonderfully beautiful.
Thank you, God.
God, you give us animals of all kinds—big and small, quiet and scary, animals for pets, animals for farms, animals in the woods, animals in the jungle.
Thank you, God.

God, you have given us other people with whom we live—
some near, some far, some like us, some very different
from us.
Thank you, God.
God, you even made each of us!
Thank you, God.
And God, you made this day when we can be together to
thank you.
Thank you, God.

The children's time in worship will conclude with the litany.

However, Pastor Mary also wants to reinforce what she intends during worship during the church school hour. She will need to elicit the cooperation of the younger children's teachers, and she has two things in mind. First, she hopes they will take the children for a walk outside and point out to the children some of the simple wonders of God's world—tree leaves, birds, flowers, the smell of fresh air, insects, and so on. These can be discussed briefly along the walk and perhaps talked about some more when the children return to their classes. Mary also hopes that the teachers will encourage the children to collect items of nature on their walk and bring them back to the classroom, where they can create a worship center and pray again the litany they used in the worship service to express their wonder and thanks for the beautiful world God has given all people. She knows such repetition can help the children to form important connections.

With her telephone calls to the children's teachers, Mary finishes planning for the teaching responsibilities that she has for the next week. Although using the same Genesis 1 text for all three teaching occasions, Mary has had to take account of many factors to plan her teaching and in the end has designed three different teaching plans. As she reflects on her work in preparing these lessons, Mary is aware of how often she is called on to teach the Bible in the church and how long it has taken her to develop the multiple skills needed to teach the Bible well. But most of all, Pastor Mary is aware of how important teaching the Bible is for the continued transformation of the church and its people, in order that they might serve God's coming reign and be faithful disciples of Jesus in their daily lives.

Summary

It is our hope that all our readers are like Pastor Mary, knowing and claiming the importance of teaching the Bible in the church with the care and intentionality it deserves. We trust that throughout all the pages of this book we have offered helpful insights for the engaging of this vital work in the community of faith. As you embrace your call to teach with hope and faith, remember that the God we come to know through the pages of scripture is the One who faithfully goes with us in all our efforts. May your teaching ministry be graced and transformed.

Women's Bible Study

Lesson Plan for Session 1:
Genesis 1—"In the Image of God"

7:00 p.m.—Welcome

- Prayer
- Introductions
- Ask women to share one thing about themselves they want the group to know.

7:10 p.m.—Focusing and Naming Current Praxis

- Read Genesis 1 aloud.
- Have Bibles available for women to follow along.
- Invite their responses.
- Play "God's Trombones."
- Invite further responses.

7:25 p.m.—Critical Reflection

- Invite participants to discuss these questions:

    How does Genesis 1 understand what it means to be human?

    How does Genesis 1 see the role of humanity in creation?

- Focus on the phrase "in the image of God," and ask women what this phrase suggests to them.

7:40 p.m.—Making Accessible the Christian Story

- Present information on the meaning of the phrase "in the image of God" in its cultural context.
- Use transparencies to help women see literary patterns in Genesis 1.
- Welcome their questions and comments.

8:05 p.m.—Integrating the Christian Story

- First in small groups and then in class as a whole, invite women to reflect on these questions:

  Do you agree that Genesis 1 builds toward day 6? What is the significance for you?

  How do you hear the claim of Genesis 1 that humanity is created in the image of God?

8:15 p.m.—Deciding/Responding

- Discuss in small groups:

  What would it mean for you to live in the image of God?

  What would it mean for us as a church to live in the image of God?

- Brief sharing as whole class

- Reminders about next week: Genesis 2—3

- Closing prayer

Notes

Introduction

[1]Walter Wink, *Transforming Bible Study*, 2d ed. (Nashville: Abingdon Press, 1989), 74.
[2]*United Church of Christ Book of Worship* (New York: United Church of Christ Office for Church Life and Leadership, 1986), 407.
[3]M. Robert Mulholland, Jr., *Shaped by the Word* (Nashville: Upper Room, 1985), 57.

Chapter 1: How We Learn

[1]Bobby McFerrin, "The 23rd Psalm," *Medicine Music*, EMI-USA CDP7-92048-2.
[2]Eric Jensen, *Teaching with the Brain in Mind* (Alexandria, Va.: ASCD, 1998), 4.
[3]Robert Sylwester, *A Celebration of Neurons: An Educator's Guide to the Human Brain* (Alexandria, Va.: ASCD, 1995), 1.
[4]Marilee Sprenger, *Learning and Memory: The Brain in Action* (Alexandria, Va.: ASCD, 1999), 2.
[5]Ibid., 3.
[6]Ibid., 56.
[7]Robert Sylwester, *A Biological Brain in a Cultural Classroom* (Thousand Oaks, Calif.: Corwin Press, 2000), 11.
[8]Sprenger, 32.
[9]Ibid., 49.
[10]Robert Sylwester, "On Using Knowledge About Our Brain," *Educational Leadership* (March 1997): 17.
[11]Jensen, 42.
[12]Carolyn R. Pool, "Maximizing Learning: A Conversation with Renate Nummela Caine," *Educational Leadership* (March 1997): 13.
[13]Jensen, 43.
[14]Ibid., 46.
[15]Ibid., 13.
[16]Renate Nummela Caine and Geoffrey Caine, *Making Connections: Teaching and the Human Brain* (Menlo Park, Calif.: Addison-Wesley, 1994), 69–70.
[17]Sprenger, 32.
[18]Jensen, 14.
[19]Jerry Larsen, *Religious Education and the Brain* (New York: Paulist Press, 2000), 97.
[20]Jensen, 100.
[21]Much of the discussion that follows draws on the work of Jensen, Larsen, and Sprenger, previously cited; Sylwester, *A Celebration of Neurons*; and Eric Jensen, *Brain-Based Learning* (San Diego: The Brain Store, 2000).
[22]Larsen, 104.
[23]See Sprenger, chapter 4.
[24]Larsen, 105.
[25]Jensen, 106.
[26]Sprenger, 53.
[27]Sprenger, 53.
[28]Ibid., 54.
[29]Marita Golden, *A Woman's Place* (Garden City, N.J.: Doubleday, 1986), 21.
[30]See Pat Burke Guild and Stephen Garger, *Marching to Different Drummers* (Alexandria, Va.: ASCD, 1998) for a helpful discussion of various ways to name and frame learning styles.
[31]Waynne James and Michael Galbraith, "Perceptual Learning Styles: Implications and Techniques for the Practitioner," *Lifelong Learning* (January 1985): 20–23.

[32]David Kolb, *Experiential Learning: Experience as the Source of Learning and Development* (Englewood Cliffs, N.J.: Prentice-Hall, 1984).

[33]Much of the material in this section is drawn from the work of Howard Gardner, *Frames of Mind: The Theory of Multiple Intelligences* (New York: Basic Books, 1983); Thomas Armstrong, *Multiple Intelligences in the Classroom* (Alexandria, Va.: ASCD, 1994); and Jerry Larsen, *Religious Education and the Brain* (New York: Paulist Press, 2000).

[34]For more information on this model and resources pertaining to it, check out www.rotation.org.

[35]Gardner's original research named seven intelligences. He has since added an eighth, naturalist intelligence, and is working on naming more. We find the original seven to be most helpful in our work on teaching the Bible and will focus our attention on these.

Chapter 2: How We Teach

[1]Parker Palmer, *The Courage to Teach: Exploring the Inner Landscape of a Teacher's Life* (San Francisco: Jossey-Bass, 1998), 2.

[2]Ibid., 3.

[3]Ibid., 10.

[4]Karen Tye, "Those Who Teach: A Qualitative Investigation of How 'Church School Teacher' Is Described and Defined by Selected Local Presbyterian Church School Teachers" (Ed.D. diss., Presbyterian School of Christian Education, 1987), 123.

[5]Ibid.

[6]Ibid., 144.

[7]Renate Nummela Caine and Geoffrey Caine, *Making Connections: Teaching and the Human Brain* (Menlo Park, Calif.: Addison-Wesley, 1994), 13.

[8]Thomas Groome, *Sharing Faith* (San Francisco: HarperSanFrancisco, 1991), 230.

[9]Tye, 82.

[10]Palmer, 11.

[11]Ibid.

[12]Jerry Larsen, *Religious Education and the Brain* (New York: Paulist Press, 2000), 48.

[13]Palmer, 2.

[14]See the following for more information on this research: Mary A. Carskadon, "An Approach to Studying Circadian Rhythms of Adolescent Humans," *Journal of Biological Rhythms* 12 (1997); Jerry Gabriel, "Sleeping In: Teens' Circadian Clocks Keep Their Own Time. Should Schools Adapt?" obtained from http://www.BrainConnection.com on December 6, 2001; and Avi Sadeh, Raviv Amiram, and Gruber Reut, "Sleep Patterns and Sleep Disruptions in School-Age Children," *Developmental Psychology* 36, no. 3 (May 2000): 291–301.

[15]To read in greater detail about Piaget's theory, see Jean Piaget and Barbel Inhelder, *The Psychology of the Child* (New York: Basic Books, 1969); and Hans Furth, *Piaget for Teachers* (Englewood Cliffs, N.J.: Prentice-Hall, 1970).

[16]Palmer, 2.

[17]Groome, 229.

[18]Elliot W. Eisner, *The Educational Imagination,* 2d ed. (New York: Macmillan, 1985), 87.

[19]Ibid.

[20]Barbara Bruce, *Our Spiritual Brain: Integrating Brain Research and Faith Development.* (Nashville: Abingdon Press, 2002), 93.

[21]Palmer, 73–83.

[22]Ibid., 74.

[23]Ibid., 75.

[24]Ibid., 76.

[25]Bruce, 97.

[26]For a full description and discussion of the shared Christian praxis approach, see Thomas Groome, *Christian Religious Education* (San Francisco: Harper & Row, 1980); and Groome, *Sharing Faith*.

[27]Groome, *Sharing Faith,* 135.

[28]For further discussion regarding the use of questions in teaching, see Donald L. Griggs, *Teaching Teachers to Teach* (Griggs Educational Service, 1974); and Richard Osmer, *Teaching for Faith* (Westminster/John Knox, 1992).

Chapter 3: An Interculural Education Experience

[1]Lesslie Newbigin, *Foolishness to the Greeks: The Gospel and Western Culture* (Grand Rapids, Mich.: Eerdmans, 1986), 4.

[2]Barbara Vacarr, "Moving Beyond Polite Correctness: Practicing Mindfulness in the Diverse Classroom," *Harvard Educational Review* 71, no. 2 (Summer 2001): 287.

[3]Mildred Sikkema and Agnes Niyekawa, *Design for Cross-Cultural Learning* (Yarmouth, Maine: Intercultural Press, 1987), 27.

[4]Milton J. Bennett, "Towards Ethnorelativism: A Developmental Model of Intercultural Sensitivity," in *Education for Intercultural Experience,* ed. R. Michael Paige (Yarmouth, Maine: Intercultural Press, 1993), 52.

[5]Edward Hall, *Beyond Culture* (Garden City, N.Y.: Anchor Books, 1977), 63.

[6]R. Michael Paige, "On the Nature of Intercultural Experiences and Intercultural Education," in *Education for Intercultural Experience,* ed. R. Michael Paige, 1.

[7]Although the shaping of these movements is our own work, we are particularly indebted to the work of Sikkema and Niyekawa, *Design for Cross-Cultural Learning,* and Milton Bennett and others in *Education for Intercultural Experience,* in helping us think about intercultural education.

[8]Sikkema and Niyekawa, 7.

[9]Newbigin, 79.

[10]Sikkema and Niyekawa, 2.

[11]For a further discussion of this, see Bennett, "Towards Ethnorelativism."

[12]Gary R. Weaver, "Understanding and Coping with Cross-Cultural Adjustment Stress," in *Education for Intercultural Experience,* ed. R. Michael Paige, 162.

[13]We are grateful to Milton J. Bennett for providing us with a framework for naming what we have observed. See Bennett, "Towards Ethnorelativism."

[14]Bennett, 45.

[15]Hall, 46.

[16]Weaver, 137.

[17]The three characteristics of Western culture or "modernity" are from Marcus Borg, *Reading the Bible Again for the First Time: Taking the Bible Seriously but Not Literally* (New York: Harper SanFrancisco, 2001), 15. For a more complete description of Western culture, see Newbigin, *Foolishness to the Greeks,* 21–41. The sketch of Western culture offered here is indebted to the helpful work of both Borg and Newbigin. Also helpful is Darrell Jodock, *The Church's Bible: Its Contemporary Authority* (Minneapolis: Fortress Press, 1989), 15–19. Jodock proposes that modernity is characterized in six ways: (1) autonomous reason, (2) progress and anti-tradition, (3) objectivity and infatuation with science, (4) optimism, (5) individualism, and (6) mechanism.

[18]Newbigin, 25–26.

[19]Borg, 16.

[20]Ibid., 17

[21]On this point, see Jodock, 71–88. Jodock identifies three characteristics of the postmodern world: (1) It lacks a sense of transcendence—that is, "the absence of any effective loyalty to something or someone beyond oneself, beyond one's nation, party, vocation, or ideology" (p. 77); (2) it lacks any overarching story—that is, "any sense of the direction in which society as a whole ought to be heading and of one's own role in its movement" (p. 79); (3) "the disappearance of societal consensus about and support for certain humane values…The loss of humane values means the readiness to inflict significant harm on others when it is politically, economically, or vocationally expedient to do so" (pp. 81–82).

[22]The colloquial use of the term *America* to refer to the United States is widespread and even evident in the title of the book on which we rely heavily in the discussion that follows (see note 24). We are aware that in significant parts of the "Americas" (North, Central, and South America) this use of *American* is seen to reflect the arrogance of the United States. Here, we use the term *American* guardedly, in the colloquial sense as a synonym for the United States, yet with keen awareness of the term's liabilities.

[23]We speak here of American culture as if it were a phenomenon. In fact, there are many American cultures. For instance, there are cultures shaped by broad regional factors (e.g., ways of living that have developed in the South or on the West coast); cultures shaped locally (e.g., the ways of living particular to the county, city, or even neighborhood where we live or where our church is located); or cultures shaped by the rich ethnic heritages in which many persons in our country

participate (e.g.,an African American culture; a variety of Latino cultures; or even, in St. Louis where the writers of this book live, a Bosnian cultural enclave).

²⁴William A. Dyrness, *How Does America Hear the Gospel?* (Grand Rapids, Mich.: Eerdmans, 1991, reprint).

²⁵Ibid., 10–27.

²⁶The following is a summary of key points made by Dyrness in a chapter titled "TheVirgin Land," 29–59.

²⁷Ibid., 50–54.

²⁸The following is a summary of key points made by Dyrness in a chapter titled "The American Dream," 60–81.

²⁹Ibid., 81.

³⁰Dyrness expresses the idea directly:"Americans are temporally optimistic." Ibid., 62.

³¹The following is a summary of key points made by Dyrness in a chapter titled "The American Adam," 82–105.

³²Ibid., 92.

³³Ibid., 78–81.

³⁴Ibid., 100–105.

³⁵In thinking about regional, local, and congregational cultures, the writings of Tex Sample are a particularly good resource—for example, *Blue-collar Ministry: Facing Economic and Social Realities of Working People* (Valley Forge, Penn.: Judson Press, 1987); and *U.S. Lifestyles and Mainline Churches: A Key to Reaching People in the 90's* (Louisville, Ky.: Westminster/John Knox Press, 1990). Sociological studies of trends in American church and religious life include Robert Wuthnow, *After Heaven: Spirituality in American Since the 1950's* (Berkeley: University of California Press, 1998), and Wade Roof, ed., *Contemporary American Religion,* 2 vols (New York: Macmillan Reference USA, 2000). Also helpful in thinking about the cultural influences that shape American church life is Robert Bellah et al., *Habits of the Heart: Individualism and Commitment in American Life* (New York: Perennial Library—Harper and Row, 1985).

³⁶Richard J. Mouw, "The Bible in Twentieth Century Protestantism: A Preliminary Taxonomy," in *The Bible in America,* ed. Nathan O. Hatch and Mark A. Noll (New York: Oxford University Press, 1982), 139.

³⁷Ibid., 144, 145, 147.

³⁸Ibid., 143.

³⁹Ibid., 144.

⁴⁰Ibid.

⁴¹Ibid., 145.

⁴²Ibid., 146.

⁴³Ibid., 147–148.

⁴⁴Ibid., 148

⁴⁵Ibid. (The quotation is from James Wallis, *Agenda for a Biblical People* [New York: Harper & Row, 1976], 69.)

⁴⁶Ibid., 149.

⁴⁷Leslie P. Hartley, *The Go-Between* (New York: Stein and Day, 1953).

⁴⁸We use this term cautiously here. Too often *strange* is a pejorative term, meaning something peculiar and negative. We use it in the sense of its primary meaning to refer to that which is previously unknown and unfamiliar.

⁴⁹Hans Walter Wolff, *Anthropology of the Old Testament,* trans. Margaret Kohl (Philadelphia: Fortress Press, 1974), 214.

⁵⁰John W. Rogerson, "Anthropology and the Old Testament," in *The World of Ancient Israel,* ed. Ronald E. Clements (Cambridge: Cambridge University Press, 1989), 17.

⁵¹George Ernest Wright, *The Biblical Doctrine of Man in Society* (London: SCM Press, 1954), 96.

Chapter 4: Issues of Interpretation

¹Daniel Patte, *The Ethics of Biblical Interpretation: A Reevaluation* (Louisville, Ky.: Westminster John Knox Press, 1995), offers important perspectives about the ethical demands of interpreting the Bible that we would commend to anyone who teaches the Bible in churches.

²Based on M. H.Abrams, *The Mirror and the Lamp* (New York: Oxford University Press, 1953), especially 3–29.

[3]For a helpful and understandable discussion of the shifts that have occurred in interpreting the Bible over the centuries, see Marcus J. Borg, *Reading the Bible Again for the First Time: Taking the Bible Seriously but Not Literally* (New York: Harper SanFrancisco, 2001), 3–20. Borg specifically discusses the Enlightenment on pp. 14ff. For a somewhat more detailed discussion of the Enlightenment, see Lesslie Newbigin, *Foolishness to the Greeks: The Gospel and Western Culture* (Grand Rapids, Mich.: William B. Eerdmans, 1986), especially 21–41. Also helpful for understanding the different ways the Bible has been interpreted through the history of the church is Justo Gonzalez, "How the Bible Has Been Interpreted in Christian Tradition," in *The New Interpreter's Bible*, vol. 1 (Nashville: Abingdon Press, 1994), 83–106.

[4]See Borg, 21–36.

[5]Ibid., 33ff. On the Bible as the word of God, see also Terence Fretheim and Karlfried Froehlich, *The Bible as Word of God in a Postmodern Age* (Minneapolis: Fortress Press, 1998). On the question of the "truth" of the Bible, we find helpful the pamphlet by William C. Placher, "Is the Bible True?" (Princeton, N.J.: Center of Theological Inquiry).

[6]For further discussion of this point, see Placher, 4–6; and Borg, 37–53.

[7]For a more complete discussion of the historical-critical approach to the Bible, see E. Krentz, *The Historical Critical Method* (Philadelphia: Fortress Press, 1975). Also see Carl C. Holladay, "Contemporary Methods of Reading the Bible," in *The New Interpreter's Bible*, vol. 1, especially 128–31. A more critical appraisal of this method is offered by Walter Brueggemann, *Theology of the Old Testament* (Minneapolis: Fortress Press, 1997), 9–15.

[8]Whereas Christians are usually comfortable referring to God as "Yahweh," in Jewish piety this name is never spoken. Instead, where the name "Yahweh" occurs in the biblical text, Jews will say "Adonai," which means "my Lord," if it is in the context of prayer and worship. In more regular speech, Jewish tradition replaces the name of God with "Ha-Shem," which means "The Name."

[9]More detailed information about the biblical books cited below is readily available. Readers may want to consult the introductory sections of commentaries in series such as *The New Interpreters Bible* (Abingdon Press) or *The Westminster Bible Companion* (Westminster John Knox Press).

[10]M. Robert Mulholland, Jr., *Shaped by the Word* (Nashville: The Upper Room, 1985), 57.

[11]Regarding these approaches that focus on the text itself in the Old Testament, see the essay "Contemporary Methods of Reading the Bible," in *The New Interpreter's Bible*, vol. 1, particularly pp. 137–43, under the heading "Features of the Literary Paradigm." A particularly instructive book on one of the interpretative approaches that focuses on the text itself is Phyllis Trible, *Rhetorical Criticism: Content, Method and the Book of Jonah,* Guides to Biblical Scholarship, ed. Gene M. Tucker (Minneapolis: Fortress Press, 1994).

[12]On the importance of focusing on the biblical text itself when teaching the Bible, see Walter Brueggemann, "That the World May Be Redescribed," *Interpretation* 56 (2002): 359–67. The synopsis that prefaces the article states: "The biblical text is itself a sufficient cause for wonder. By using an exegetical method that focuses resolutely upon the text, teachers can help people find themselves addressed and reimagined by this 'strange new world' of the Bible" (359).

[13]This phrase appears in days two, four, five, and six, but is absent from days one and three.

[14]The word "separate" does not occur in days three and six.

[15]"Dominion" can be easily misunderstood as a charge that gives humanity license to exploit other creatures and God's creation. The sense of the word "dominion" is probably akin to the way this word is used in Psalm 72. In the psalm the dominion of the king (v. 8) is closely tied to the king's responsibility to care for those who are weak and marginalized (vv. 1–4, 12–14). Thus, dominion is best understood to suggest the need to be a caretaker of the creation, with particular concern for those parts of the creation most vulnerable and open to exploitation. See Walter Brueggemann, *Genesis,* Interpretation Series (Atlanta: Westminster John Knox Press, 1986), 32–35; Terence Fretheim, "The Book of Genesis," in *The New Interpreter's Bible*, vol. 1, 346; or W. Sibley Towner, *Genesis,* Westminster Companion to the Bible (Louisville: Westminster John Knox Press, 2001), 28–29.

[16]For instance, see Fretheim, "The Book of Genesis," 341.

[17]Regarding the use of the Bible with children, we find particularly instructive the work of A. Roger and Gertrude G. Gobbel, *The Bible: A Children's Playground* (Philadelphia: Fortress Press, 1986). Also helpful for teaching the Bible to both children and youth is Iris Cully, *The Bible in Christian Education* (Minneapolis: Fortress Press, 1995), 69–95.

[18]We raised this issue briefly at the beginning of this chapter. See Patte, *The Ethics of Biblical Interpretation.*

[19]For a sampling of the variety of interpretative approaches that focus on the reader of biblical texts, see Susan E. Gillingham, *One Bible, Many Voices: Different Approaches to Biblical Studies* (Grand Rapids, Mich.: Eerdmans, 1998), particularly the bibliography, 248–70. Here are a few examples of books reflecting this approach that we have found helpful: Cain Hope Felder, *Stony the Road We Trod: African American Biblical Interpretation* (Minneapolis: Fortress Press, 1991); Carol A. Newsom and Sharon Ringe, eds., *The Women's Bible Commentary* (Louisville: Westminster/John Knox Press, 1992); Letty Russell, ed., *Feminist Interpretation of the Bible* (Philadelphia: Westminster Press, 1985); Elsie Tamez, *The Amnesty of Grace* (Eugene, Oreg.: Wiph and Stock Publishers, 2002); Luise Schottroff, Silvia Schroer, and Marie-Theres Wacker, *Feminist Interpretation: The Bible in Women's Perspective,* trans. Martin and Barbara Rumscheidt (Minneapolis: Fortress Press, 1998); Fernando F. Segovia and Mary Ann Tolbert, eds., *Teaching the Bible: The Discourses and Politics of Biblical Pedagogy* (Maryknoll, N.Y.: Orbis Press, 1998); Phyllis Trible, *God and the Rhetoric of Sexuality* (Minnneapolis: Fortress Press, 1978).

[20]Alice Laffey, *The Pentateuch: A Liberation-Critical Reading* (Minneapolis: Fortress Press, 1998), 3.

[21]Ibid., 12.

[22]Ibid.

[23]Again, we use the word *strange* guardedly. See chapter 3, note 48.

Chapter 5: Putting It All Together

[1]A recording of James Weldon Johnson's "God's Trombones, The Creation" is available on the CD *Voices of Black America* (Naxos #22481, 2002), disc 1, track 9.